Asian Elements

Graphic Design in the East

SANDU

Asian Elements

Graphic Design in the East

Edited and produced by
Sandu Publishing Co., Ltd.

Sponsored by Design 360°
– Concept & Design Magazine

Book design, concept & art direction by
Sandu Publishing Co., Ltd.
Publisher: Sandu Publishing Co., Ltd.
Chief Editor: Wang Shaoqiang
Executive Editor: Zhang Zhonghui
Design Director: Wang Shaoqiang
Designer: Huang Zhiyi
Sales Managers: Niu Guanghui (China), Winnie Feng (International)

Front cover projects by YOULIYOUJIE™, Ta Quang Huy, TICK.DESIGN,
Sun Shine, Shawn Goh Graphic Design Lab., TOMSHI AND ASSOCIATES
Back cover projects by Asthetíque Group, 1983ASIA,
TOMSHI AND ASSOCIATES, GM creative
Cover Design: Pan Yuhua, Huang Zhiyi

info@sandupublishing.com
sales@sandupublishing.com
www.sandupublishing.com
weibo.com/sandupublishing

Published by Sandu Publishing Co., Ltd.
Address: 5th Floor, Wah Kit Commercial Centre, 302 Des Voeux Road Central,
Hong Kong

Size: 210mm × 285mm
First Edition: 2019

ISBN 978-988-78528-1-0

Printed and bound in China

CONTENTS

PREFACE

By 1983ASIA

People always endow some certain meanings into the things they create, this is a prevalent phenomenon amongst the Asian, like they would do it at their cores. In Ang Lee's movie, an old shirt can carry the deepest feeling of missing someone, while beaches and rivers are always metaphor something in Kim Ki-duk's films; in the West, bat is equal to vampire which means evil, but in China, bat is a symbol of good luck because the homophone pronunciation in Chinese; Japanese use pitchforks as New Year's decoration, because "pitchforks" in Japanese sounds like "bear's paw" which can grasp the good fortune.

In Indian's wedding ceremony, the bride's hands are drawn with traditional patterns: birds are symbolize man's energy, fish are symbolize woman's fertility. These are blessings of many children. In Chinese wedding, couple are wearing "Dragon and Phoenix" costume, which means transforming the energy of dragon and phoenix and bringing richness... Asian people metaphor what they saw, what they listened, and what they comprehended into their stories, and then tell the world about them. Asian stories are fascinating. Although with the development of modern civilization, stories are become more like ancient tales and cannot transmit the deeper context correctly. But indeed, this is what keeps Asian special and unique.

We say that "designer" is like "translator", they both translate the origin of matter and thought, in a visual way. This whole world is like a platform that full of cultural conflicts. Even if we talk in different languages, have various cultural backgrounds, we still can obtain information and inspiration through our eyes. In all ages, we read the foreign classic literature through the language translator, and cultural export Chinese works so that people on the platform get to know each other. Different cultural communications require a text translator, and of course, a visual translator, which is also the duty and mission for the designer.

Design and modern business are inseparable. Business is related to everyone's life, and culture is the base of design. They are impact on each other. How to balance these aspects is a problem that designer has to deal with. Ancient stories exist in historical era, they are parts of the culture; yet culture does not only exist in history, it stays around us, it changes with the time. *Asian Elements - Graphic Design in the East* translates modern design in a visual way. It's a challenge and also a responsibility. It continues the story-telling and present a better world for us. We believe, this is probably another way of heritage.

As the largest, most populous continent, Asia is rich in resources. Cultures of different regions are diverse from each other. This book is dedicated to present the varied cultural elements of Asia.

Lotus

Design: 1983ASIA

* *Lotus is symbolize elegance and decency in China. Zhang Xiaogang, a Chinese famous painter, is skillful in lotus painting. Lotus has diverse postures and emotions in his artworks. They are reflection of his different spirits and growths. This design is attempt to get closer to the artist's mind.*

Gemfavor Food is a traditional food brand. It sticks to the quality and endows food with another life. Brand, consumer and artist, these three characters are connect with each other. They match the conception of "everything is connected and life will last long". For 1983ASIA, "ingenuity" vs "originality" means that two persistent minds should appreciate each other. Just like the lotus enjoy the glorious moon in the water along with its inverted reflection, they connect each other beyond time and space. Based on this, 1983ASIA has created a "scene": Bathing in the moonlight, beautiful lotus are blossoming in the tranquil water. They have found the other half of spirit and complete themselves.

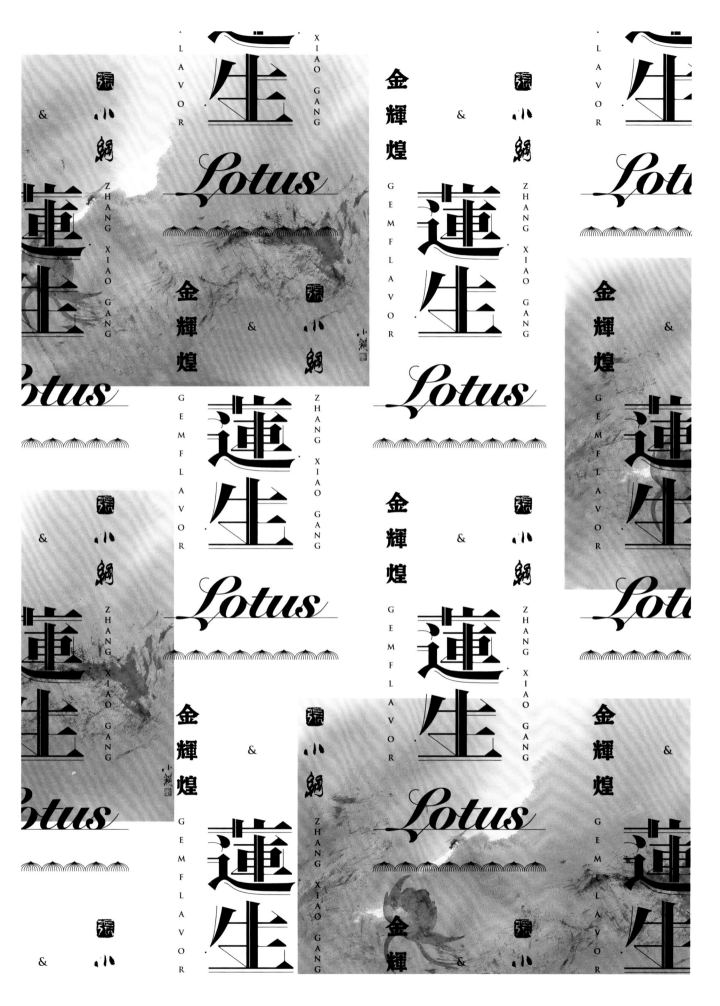

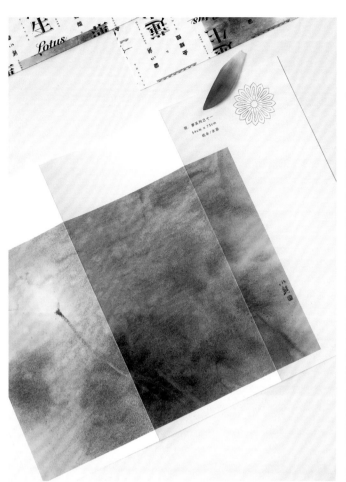

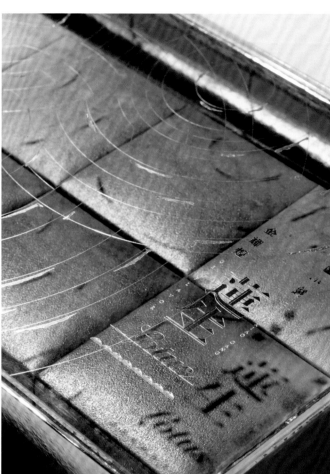

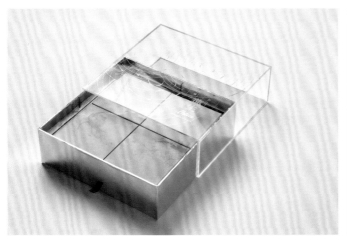

Cai Zhi Zhai

Design: Li Jialing

* Most of the Classical Gardens of Suzhou are built by scholars, standardized many of the key features of classical Chinese garden design with constructed landscapes mimicking natural scenery of rocks, hills and rivers with strategically located pavilions and pagodas.

This is a packaging designed for a gift box of Suzhou traditional deserts. The specialty lies in the combination of 2D graphic and 3D structure. The key is to evoke customers' memories and their resonation. Designer incorporates both characteristic of the Classical Gardens of Suzhou, which is white walls and black-tiled roofs, and her childhood memory of playing hide-and-seek within into the package design.

Little Tokyo

Design: KittoKatsu

....

* Traditional Japanese maneki-neko and German (Rhineland) symbolism combined with graphic elements and a strong color palette are applied in this work.

The city of Düsseldorf has one of the biggest Japanese communities in Europe. Little Tokyo is the vibrant center of the city's Japanese cultural life. The goal of this project was to create an identity that would give the district a strong and independent voice. By mixing traditional elements of Japanese culture such as the maneki-neko (welcoming cat) with typical Rhineland icons like the Altbier (old beer), the identity reflects the unique cultural fusion that is characteristic of the district. Used with a palette of bold colors and strong typographic elements, it becomes playful yet respectful of heritage and culture.

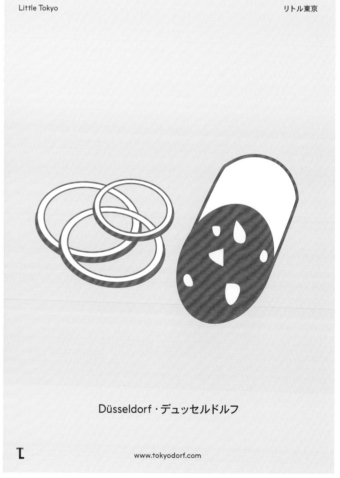

Viên - Full Moon Festival

Design: Hoa Nguyen (AJ)

Circle in Vietnamese is "Viên", which belongs to the term "Đoàn Viên", means family gathering. It is not only represents the round things, like moon, cake, lantern, round table, etc, but also stands for wholeness, fullness, and togetherness.

Designer uses the circles to illustrate different moments of human life, especially the activities of moon cake packaging on the Full Moon Festival. The packaging becomes a medium to confirm the existence of the circles around us and link them with the concept of togetherness. Therefore, every time people see a circle, that basic shape can remind them about the family, the reunion and the love among them all.

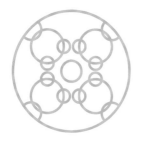   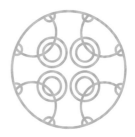

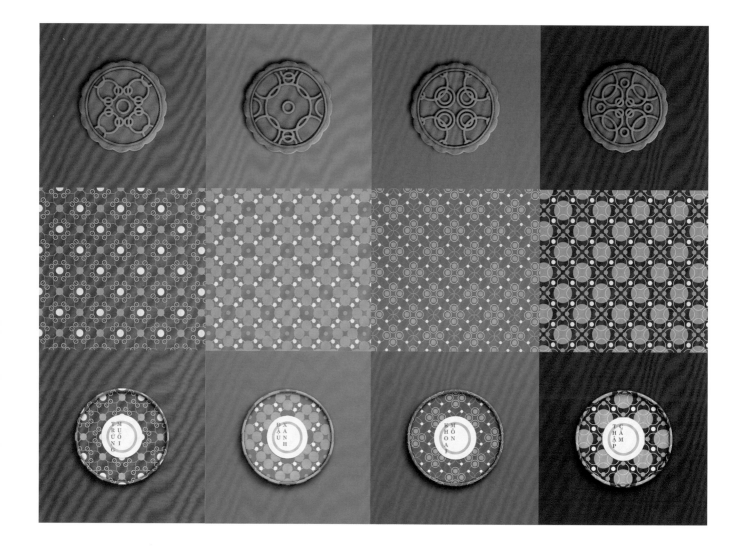

The Sachet Codes

Design: Miao Shou Hui Chao

During the Chinese Warring States period a scented sachet was an ornament worn on the body and used to absorb sweat, repel insects and ward off evils. In the Han Dynasty both boys and girls wore sachets and in the Tang Dynasty and Song Dynasty scented bags gradually became preferred only by women. A scented sachet became a love token in the Qing Dynasty.

Designers summarized the main patterns of sachets in ancient times, and found that the patterns are different from people who wore. So based on the crowd, they divided the sachets into several groups: for the old, children, men, and women. They use the patterns to send messages. For example, in ancient time, "bee" symbolizes man, hence, the sachet for man is decorated with bee pattern.

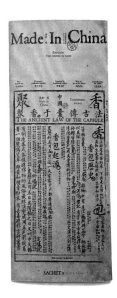

Milk Trade

Design: And A Half Branding
and Design Studio
Photography: Tarish Zamora

....

** This design is inspired from traditional
Chinese medicine packaging, old-fashioned
illustrations, and classic items.*

Milk Trade is a dessert store that specializes
in authentic Hong Kong street fare. The
entire menu consists of several flavors of
steamed milk, Hong Kong style egg waffles,
and milk tea.

Chinese outdated arts, dynasty portraits,
and a strong sense of auspiciousness were
the main influences for the brand. Through
Chinglish, regality, and beauty, Milk Trade
evokes the streets of Hong Kong and
the culture embedded in these Chinese
delicacies.

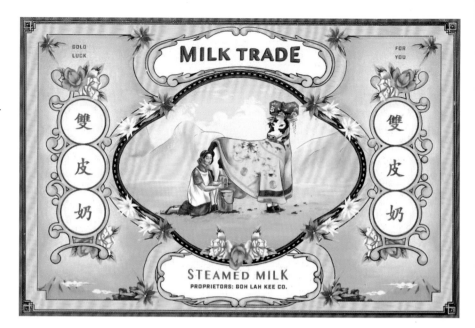

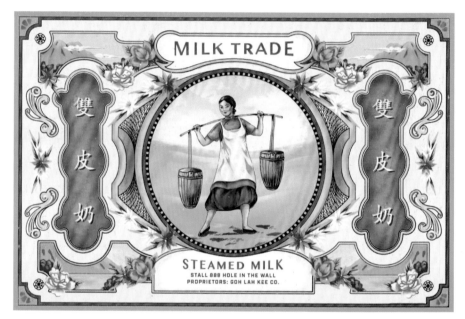

Chang

Design: Estudio Yeyé   **Photography:** Raúl Villalobos

* A mixture of different elements from Asia, such as Thailand's Buddhism, Japanese animation, Chinese celebrity, and many more.

Chang is a Thai restaurant which is influenced by other Asian cultures. This mix gives Estudio Yeyé the opportunity to blend thousands of visual elements from every corner of the Asian domain. Lights, tigers, unusual customs and thousands of flavors, create a unique atmosphere. Chang will guide the visitor to an unknown place, take them into a time zone when adventurous eating was appreciated.

Shyun Ramen Bar

Design: Hue Studio   **Photography:** Jave Lee

*** This work uses Japanese calligraphy and sea wave patterns as the main elements.**

Shyun means "season" in Japanese. It is their commitment to only using the freshest, seasonal ingredients in crafting their ramen. True to their Japanese heritage, the Shyun Ramen Bar branding incorporates the Japanese wave hand painted in calligraphic brush to provide the authentic experience with the casualness of an izakaya style.

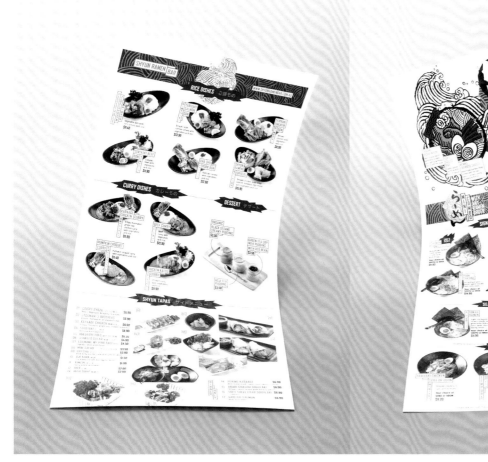

Oil-Paper Umbrella

Design: Yi-Hsuan Li

....

* Oil-paper umbrella is a type of paper umbrella that originated from China. It subsequently spread across Asia, to Japan, Korea, Vietnam, Malaysia, Thailand and Laos. People in these countries have further developed the oil-paper umbrella with different characteristics.

Oil-paper umbrella is extremely beautiful, it's not only a symbol of Chinese culture but also have a long history. Designers apply the design with simply few colors and elements which is consistent with the concise style of oil-paper umbrella. Regarding the design details, they slightly adjust the font "Adobe Ming Std L" and "AR Roman" as main typography. Umbrella elegant motifs and detailed structures are very suitable with these two fonts since they have the same elements: delicate strokes and glamorous curves. When it comes to colors, there are blue, orange and black. Sky blue and sun orange are symbol colors of MEI-NONG in designer's memory. Few oranges in a large blue area make canvas warmer and vivacious.

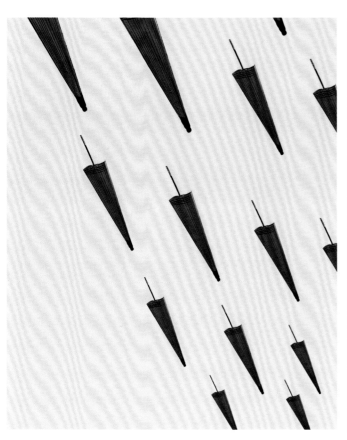

MEI NONG
OIL-PAPER UMBRELLA

Oil-paper umbrella have been the cultural symbol of the Hakka in Meinong District of Kaoshiung. The production procedures are divided to five major portions. This include the umbrella scaffold, umbrella production, umbrella head, umbrella handle and art painting. With any one of the above been done, the umbrella could be called as a "full art".

FIVE STEPS TO MAKE AN OIL-PAPER UMBRELLA

STEP 1 Bamboo is selected.
STEP 2 The bamboo is crafted and soaked in water. It is then dried in the sun, drilled, threaded and assembled into a skeleton.
STEP 3 Paper is cut and glued onto the skeleton. It is trimmed, oiled, and exposed to sunlight.
STEP 4 Lastly, patterns are painted onto the umbrella.

Oil-paper umbrella (Chinese: 油紙傘) is a type of paper umbrella that originated from China. It subsequently spread across Asia, to Japan, Korea, Vietnam, Malaysia, Thailand and Laos. People in these countries have further developed the oil paper umb rella with different characteristics. As the Hakka moved to Taiwan, the oil-paper umbrella also began to develop in Taiwan. [1]

Hakka

美濃油紙傘

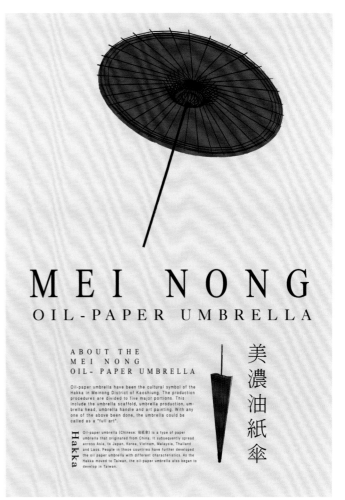

MEI NONG
OIL-PAPER UMBRELLA

ABOUT THE MEI NONG OIL-PAPER UMBRELLA

Oil-paper umbrella have been the cultural symbol of the Hakka in Meinong District of Kaoshiung. The production procedures are divided to five major portions. This include the umbrella scaffold, umbrella production, umbrella head, umbrella handle and art painting. With any one of the above been done, the umbrella could be called as a "full art".

Oil-paper umbrella (Chinese: 油紙傘) is a type of paper umbrella that originated from China. It subsequently spread across Asia, to Japan, Korea, Vietnam, Malaysia, Thailand and Laos. People in these countries have further developed the oil-paper umbrella with different characteristics. As the Hakka moved to Taiwan, the oil-paper umbrella also began to develop in Taiwan.

Hakka

美濃油紙傘

Feng He

Design: 1983ASIA

* In Chinese culture, "wind" embodies Chinese people's wisdom and elegance, "crane" represents a high position in eastern culture, especially red-crowned crane, it's a symbol of longevity and good luck. It is used to be linked with the immortals, also known as "immortal crane".

Feng He is an independent high-end new Chinese home brand. 1983ASIA combined abstract "wind" and figurative "crane" and used expression technique to design an exquisite and cursive script. They also re-painted the dancing image of "auspicious crane", which learns from the ancient paintings. This design has produced an oriental charm that beyond expression. In order to mix art and culture into the brand, 1983ASIA made bold attempt to interpret the traditional Chinese saying "there are pictures in the book and books within the picture", and combined some simple and neat modern text design together.

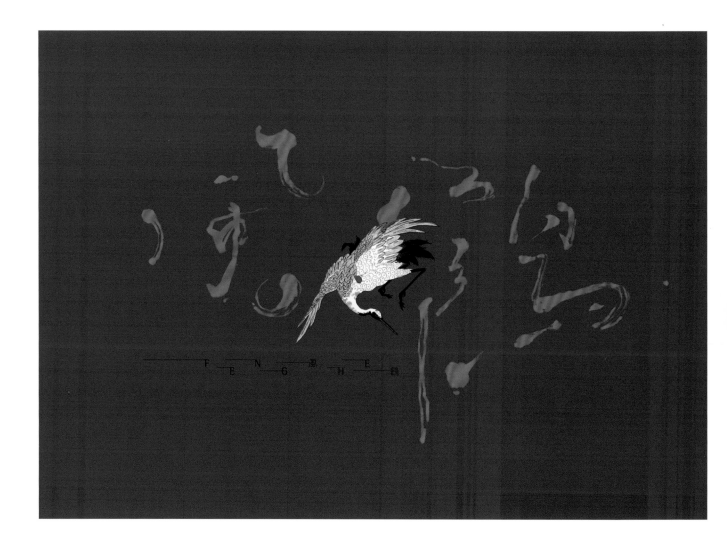

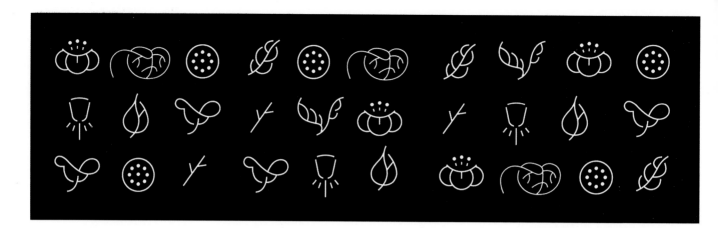

Lotus Tea

Design: GM creative

* *This work presents Vietnam's traditional tea-picking industry.*

Lotus tea (tra sen) is believed to be represented for the Vietnamese tea culture ever since the ancient time and still now spreading all over the world. Lotus tea itself has a spiritual meaning in Vietnamese tea culture at philosophy, courtesy and esteem levels.

CHỌN NHỮNG LÁ TRÀ TƯƠI XANH NHẤT

VÒ TƠI

SẤY TRÀ THỦ CÔNG

THƯỞNG THỨC TRÀ SEN

KHAI SÁNG TRÍ TUỆ

ĐÀM LUẬN CÁI ĐẠO Ở ĐỜI

GÁNH TRÀ LÀ NÉT ĐẸP LAO ĐỘNG, THỂ HIỆN SỨC MẠNH HÌNH THỂ CŨNG NHƯ TINH THẦN LAO ĐỘNG CẦN CÙ CỦA NGƯỜI DÂN VIỆT. VÌ VẬY UỐNG TRÀ KHÔNG CHỈ LÀ NÉT ĐẸP THƯỞNG THỨC MÀ CÒN LÀ SỰ HƯỞNG THỤ THÀNH QUẢ CỦA SỨC LAO ĐỘNG, LÒNG QUYẾT TÂM, SỰ KIÊN NHẪN TRONG MỖI CON NGƯỜI.

LỰC ĐIỀN
GÁNH TRÀ

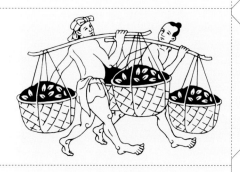

Tsui Wah Restaurant

Design: Margaret Cheung

* Elements in this work include nostalgic culture in Hong Kong and traditional Chinese cuisine.

Tsui Wah Restaurant has a long history and has witnessed the changes in Hong Kong during the past fifty years. This work is mainly based on the old characteristic elements of Hong Kong, and presents the nostalgia culture with photo collage. In addition, slang is widely used as a theme to show the culture of Hong Kong nostalgic tea restaurant.

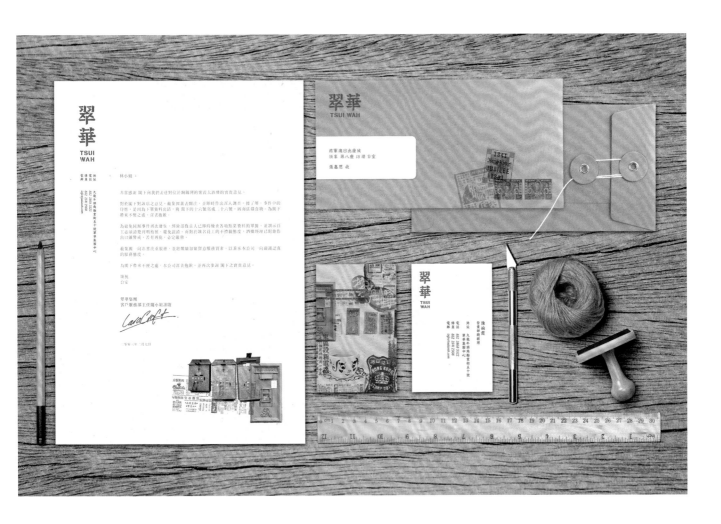

World Partner Forum

Design: Paperlux Studio
Creative Direction: Max Kuehne
Photography: Michael Pfeiffer

....

** Elements in this work include mahjong, paper cutting, and
landmark buildings of Beijing, Xi'an and Shanghai.*

In 2016, the World Partner Forum asked Paperlux Studio to head
to Beijing, Xi'an and Shanghai to create a unique experience for
their guests. The key visual was designed to be quite modular—
there was one for the whole trip as well as one for each city.
Daimler Financial Services' guests received invitations with a
uniquely cut diorama, made solely out of paper. It also included
personalized chopsticks, hinting at the culinary highlights of
the trip. And the trip guide "Nice To Meet You" was an almost
traditionally sought after book. Upon arrival guests also found
the unique design on the "Do not disturb" signs for their rooms,
good night letters, presents, menu cards etc. The trip will remain
unforgettable for guests, host and Paperlux.

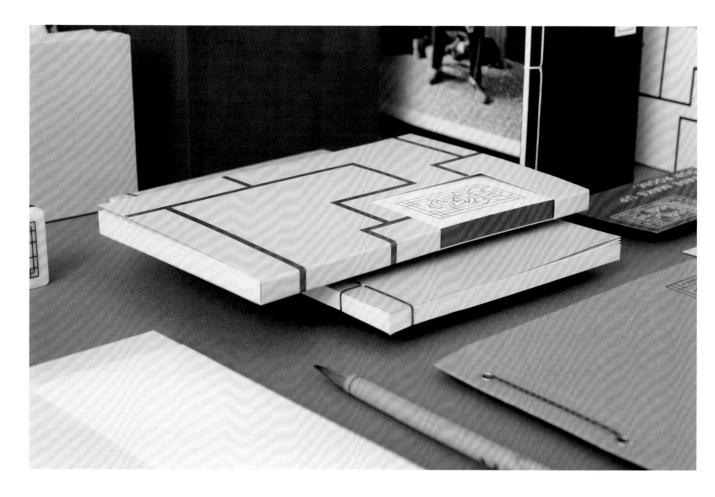

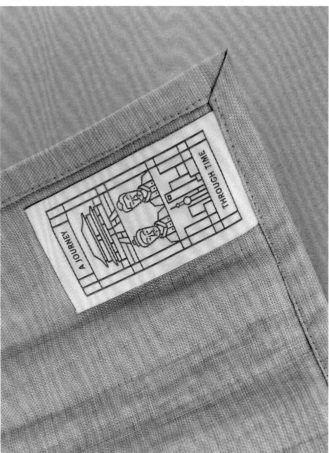

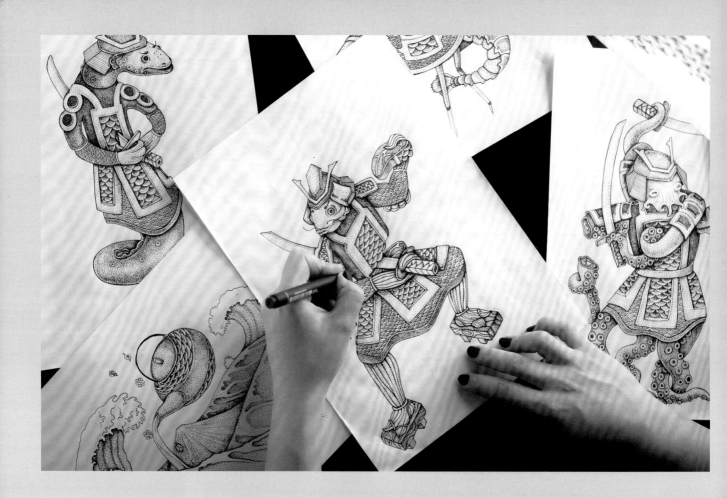

Samurai Japanese Cuisine

Design: MAROG Creative Agency   **Photography:** Arnos Martirosyan

* Samurai were the military nobility and officer caste of medieval and early-modern Japan.

The team came up with the idea of samurai fish who commit hara-kiri to satisfy their Emperors. This unusual Japanese ritual and the peculiarities of Japanese cuisine inspired the designers to create four characters of self-sacrificing fishes. A Latin font was stylized to create a visual connection with Japanese calligraphy and to pass on a taste of Japan. The color blue emphasizes the freshness of the fish. Black and grey point to the premium quality and price aspect of the brand.

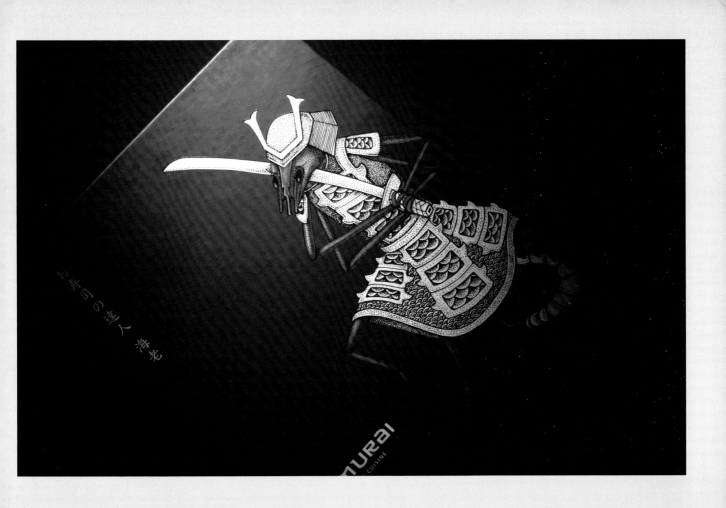

Taikin

Design: Oscar Bastidas

* Yōkai are a class of supernatural monsters, spirits, and demons in Japanese folklore.

Taikin means "fortune" in English, it is also linked to the Tanuki, this character is the main part of the "graphic story" that is told in the restaurant, a branding design full of illustrations and details. A detailed investigation was made of the Yōkai, mythological beings of Japanese culture who have existed for centuries with really interesting stories and with an important impact on their society and culture.

Fu Chung

Design: Victor Branding Design Corp.

* The military dependent's village has been a special building and living style of Taiwan, China, between 1949 and 1960s, carrying the growth memories and life experience of many people. It is also a valuable cultural asset.

Fu Chung intends to promote the savor of military dependents' village in Taiwan, China, through the food. The concept stresses the weight of brand identity in Chinese. The image of chopsticks is used to highlight the most common cooking style in military dependents' village. The eye-catching red bricks are used to convey the emotional attachment and delicacy of hometown. Within the product system, the Chinese-English wording regulatory system was reconstructed to ensure the alignment of its presentation to consumers.

Tsutori

Design: TICK.DESIGN

* The identity created for the Tsutori Japanese restaurant is inspired by the most iconic Japanese torii.

The Japanese style is outstanding from the logo design to the store design. The brand patterns are composed of different styles of torii and applied to a variety of items, capturing the guests' attention with exquisite and unique Japanese style. The overall brand image is integrated and highlights the spirit of attention to details. The restaurant is dedicated to bringing a unique Japanese cuisine experience to the guests. Tsutori is undoubtedly the choice of satisfaction.

The Method of Heaven & Earth to Restore Lost Qi   **Design:** Ta Quang Huy

* Traditional Chinese Medicine is built on a foundation of more than 2,500 years of Chinese medical practice that includes various forms of herbal medicine, acupuncture, massage, exercise, and dietary therapy.

As Western lifestyle is prominent in the Asian everyday life, people eat and sleep a lot and they also take too many pills to cure their diseases. Among other things, this leads to antibiotic resistance in the long term. The book invites the readers to study Traditional Chinese Medicine, more precisely the two philosophies: Yin and Yang, and Wuxing. The ancient sages teach human beings to be able to preserve their energy and balance their blood so that evil energy cannot penetrate their bodies.

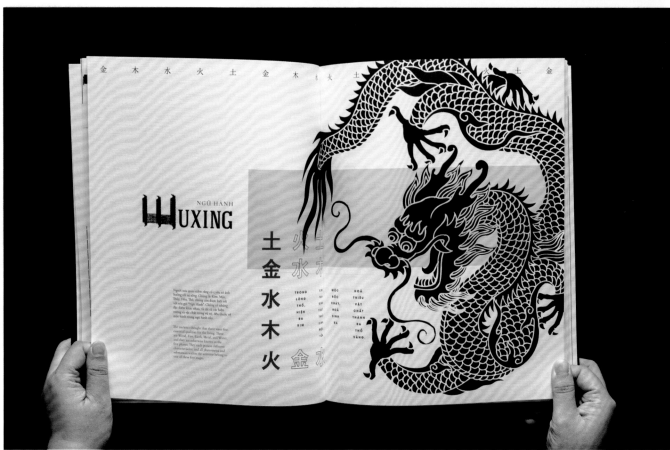

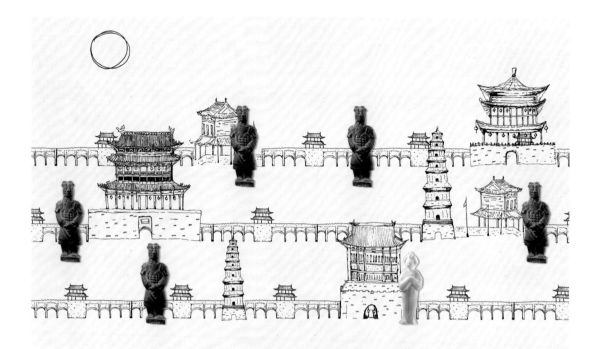

Shaanxi Thirteen

Design: Victor Branding Design Corp.

* Shaanxi is considered one of the cradles of Chinese civilization. Thirteen feudal dynasties established their capitals in the province during a span of more than 1,100 years, from the Zhou Dynasty to the Tang Dynasty.

All customs originate from the changes of the four seasons. In addition to the embedding of the architecture of the ancient city and the scenery spots, the miniature images of the four seasons are installed in. The surprises are kept in the shelves, while the long historical elegance is prolonged till now. Every single box packaging is based on the principle of lightweight hand-held convenience. The handles are styled in alignment with the walls, creating the unique identification of the brand. The gift box uses brick-red colors, not only giving its festivity image, but also displaying the strong color impression of Xi'an. With the reduction of packaging materials, Victor managed to acquire the perfect balance between aesthetics, ecology and convenience of the brand.

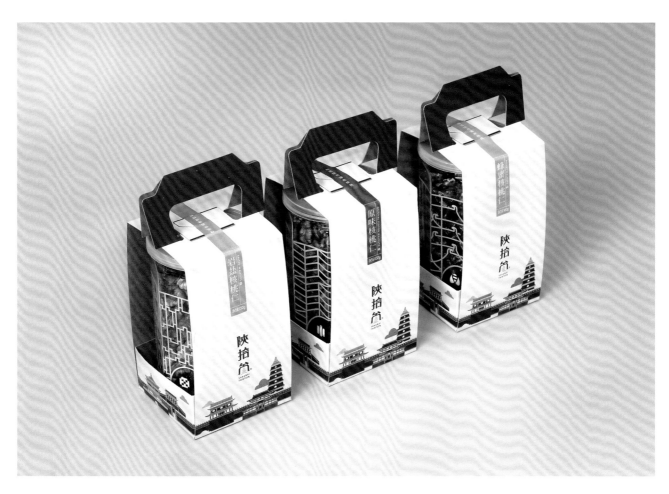

鵸鵌

舟遺魚

鯈魚

耳鼠

Shan Hai Medicated Wine

Design: Xiaoyue Liu

The Classic of Mountains and Seas, also known as Shan Hai Jing, is a Chinese classic text and a compilation of mythic geography and myth.

Medicated wine is obtained by mixing wine and Chinese medicinal herbs together through certain processes. The earliest records can be found in oracle bone inscriptions of the Shang Dynasty. The production and application of medicated wine is valued by physicians of all dynasties. A lot of recipes are still being used today to treat illness or serve as a supplement to healthy life style. The packaging is inspired by *The Classic of Mountains and Seas.* Each illustrated creature has its unique therapeutic effect according to the text.

2016 Chinese New Year Card   **Design:** Chieh-ting Lee

* *Designer composed New Year scroll, fire crack, the Spring and lantern to be iconic symbols.*

In the year of the Monkey, designer took the figure of monkey into the type " 猴 " and other illustrations. In Chinese culture, gold and red colors represent that good fortune is coming. However, in some regions of Asia, they have different meanings. Designer tried different colors of paper, like black and white with gold foil stamping. This has highlighted the work in different background and showed the elegant printing effect.

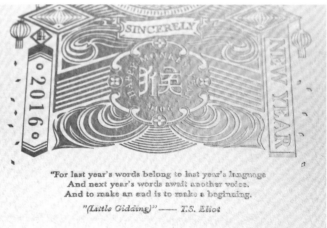

Dong Rice

Design: Zhang Han

The Dong people, also known as Kam people, a Kam-Sui people of southern China, are one of the 56 ethnic groups officially recognized by the People's Republic of China.

Dong Rice is a local brand based on the side of Duliu River, Qiandongnan. It still persists in the traditional Dong's labor way today, and hopes to bring more people to the birthplace of Dong rice. The packaging employs simple style, and through hand drawing, repeated engraving and rubbing, it has obtained different scenes and themes.

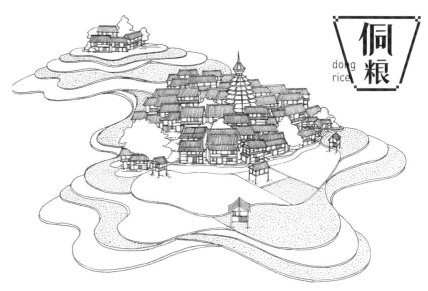

Indra

Design: Zhang Han

....

* This work is inspired by Chongqing's hot pot.

This brand adheres to authentic taste and handmade exclusive. Designer hopes to share people with the brand's insistence on material. Every day in the mountain city, Chongqing, ingredients and basic materials are airlifted to reprocessing. For those foreign diners, Indra may be a home to the food memory, or a mountain city with unlimited daydream. The graphic line visual representation is about to link the flavors with senses.

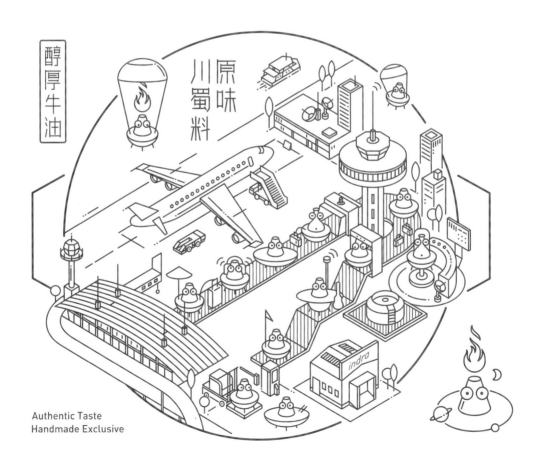

Authentic Taste
Handmade Exclusive

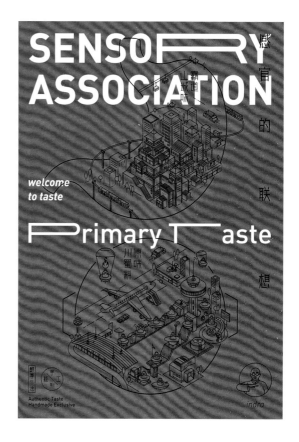

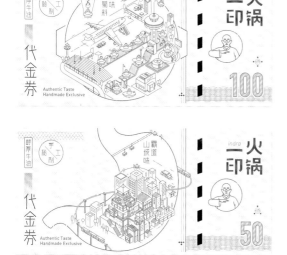

Four Generations Under One Roof

Design: Rong Brand

"Four generations under one roof" is a Chinese idiom, it means an ideal family. It also represents "happiness", "affluence", "longevity", and "joy". Corresponding fruits are pomegranate, cucurbit, peach and persimmon. Also, "four generations" in Chinese pronunciation is "si shi", equal to "four lions".

Designers replace the original knitting balls under lions feet with four fruits—pomegranate, cucurbit, peach and persimmon, then convert the kerosene lamp and repeat the pattern to stand for family lights. They also play the idioms solitaire game and apply plaque elements in the design. Rong Brand is aim at forging the top dinning brand in Beijing.

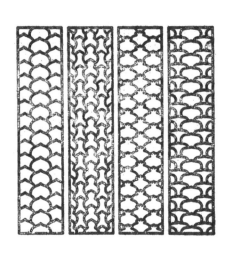

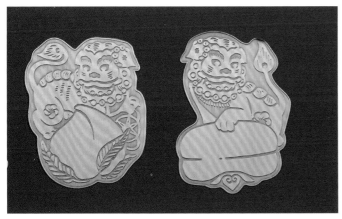

The Monkey King's Gift Box

Design: Miao Shou Hui Chao

* The Monkey King is a figure who features in a body of legends, which can be traced back to the period of the Song Dynasty. He appears as a main character in the 16th century Chinese classical novel Journey to the West.

Designers put the idea of *Havoc in Heaven* into the couplets, and upgrade the composed character. They use golden cudgel as the main packaging and take the Monkey King as spokesman of the gift box. The calendar and red packet are placed together as one. Have fun with the Monkey King on the new year!

Red Envelopes

Design: 9 × 9. Design

This work applies the Chinese traditional pattern such as magpies, fans, flowers and grass, quadrilateral and other Chinese elements with an interesting and modern typesetting methods to the design.

New year's gift box is not only a blessing, but also an important way to convey the brand culture. As an extension of the new image of brand upgrading, ALT New Year's gift box must be combined with fashion and tradition to deduce the traditional materials to a sense of fashion. The brand color of bright blue, with the of laser technology, gives this design more sense of science and fashion.

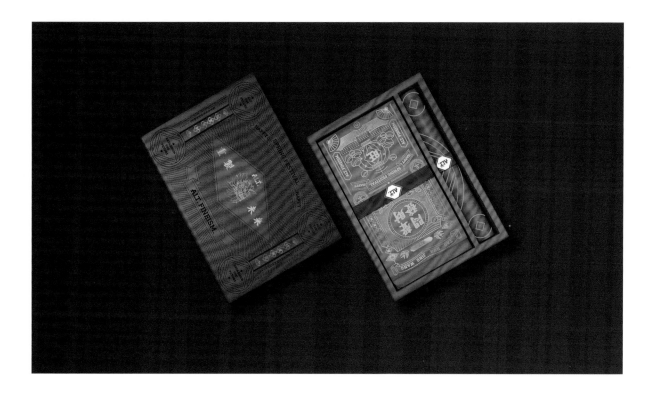

45 Symbols

Design: Chieh-ting Lee

* Chinese traditional religion is polytheistic; many deities are worshipped in a pantheistic view where divinity is inherent in the world. The gods are energies or principles revealing, imitating and propagating the way of Heaven.

This project is intended to represent the idea of combining the traditional gods into contemporary life which is connect with people's daily life, and to remind people what the gods may be responsible for. Hence, people can ask for blessings accordingly.

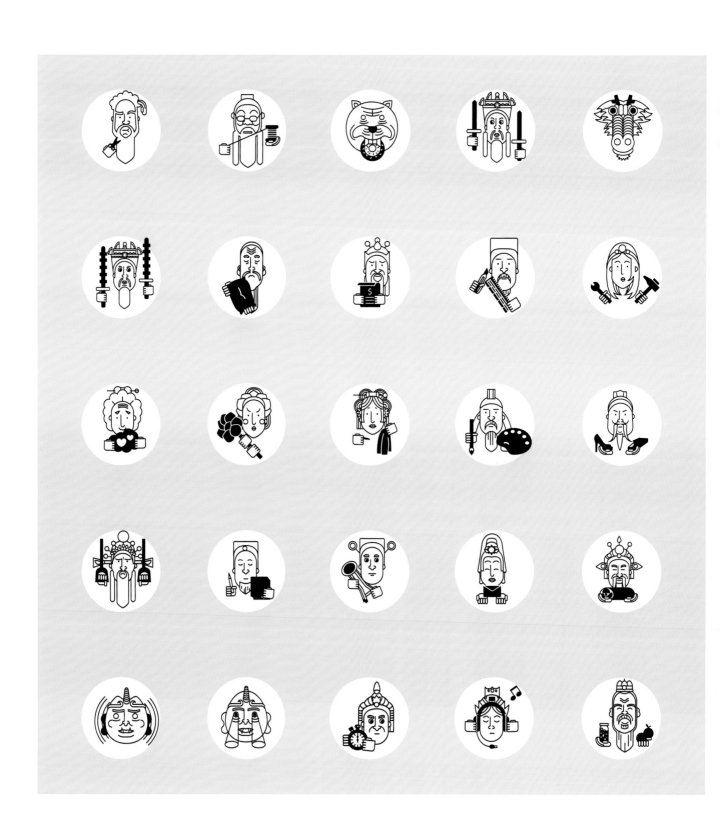

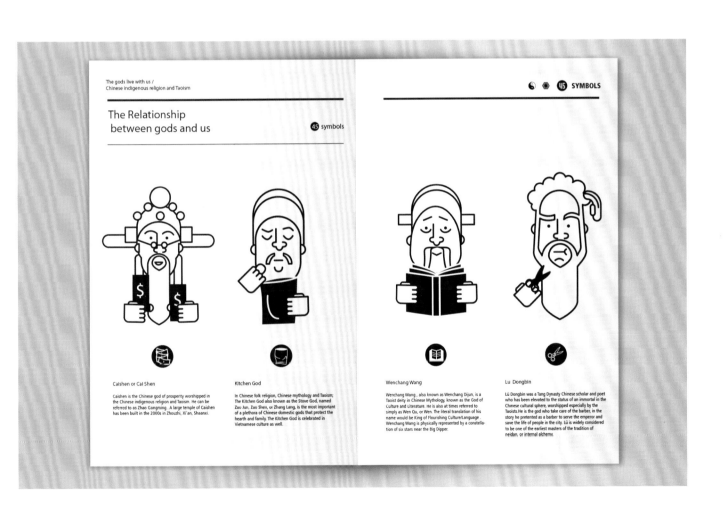

The gods live with us /
Chinese indigenous religion and Taoism

SYMBOLS

The Relationship
between gods and us

45 symbols

Caishen or Cai Shen

Caishen is the Chinese god of prosperity worshipped in the Chinese indigenous religion and Taoism. He can be referred to as Zhao Gongming . A large temple of Caishen has been built in the 2000s in Zhouzhi, Xi'an, Shaanxi.

Kitchen God

In Chinese folk religion, Chinese mythology and Taoism; The Kitchen God also known as the Stove God, named Zao Jun, Zao Shen, or Zhang Lang, is the most important of a plethora of Chinese domestic gods that protect the hearth and family. The Kitchen God is celebrated in Vietnamese culture as well.

Wenchang Wang

Wenchang Wang , also known as Wenchang Dijun, is a Taoist deity in Chinese Mythology, known as the God of Culture and Literature. He is also at times referred to simply as Wen Qu, or Wen. The literal translation of his name would be King of Flourishing Culture/Language . Wenchang Wang is physically represented by a constellation of six stars near the Big Dipper.

Lu Dongbin

Lü Dongbin was a Tang Dynasty Chinese scholar and poet who has been elevated to the status of an immortal in the Chinese cultural sphere, worshipped especially by the Taoists.He is the god who take care of the barber, in the story he pretended as a barber to serve the emperor and save the life of people in the city. Lü is widely considered to be one of the earliest masters of the tradition of neidan, or internal alchemy.

Industrious Towel Factory

Design: Rong Brand

* *Classical Chinese garden window is the highlight in the brand.*

This design is about to create a retro visual effect of old factory during the republic of China period. The symbol of the brand is the classical Chinese garden windows. And the logo is a view of a working woman's back. This is symbolizes producer is the spokesman of Industrious Towel Factory. Rong Brand is about to build up a brand that full of Chinese characteristics and aesthetics.

Dog Brain Tea

Design: UNIDEA BANK
Photography: Chen Yue, Huang Renqiang

* Shennong is a mythological Chinese deity in Chinese folk religion and venerated as a mythical sage ruler of prehistoric China. He tastes amount of herbs by himself to test toxicity.

The dog brain logo refers to the historical myth of Shennong tasting herbs. With the vivid imitation of tea in the Kylin dog's mouth, it reflects the profound culture of the tea. This makes the dog brain logo more impressive, and the classic color scheme makes the whole design more distinguished.

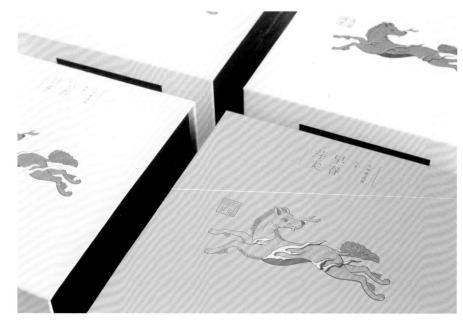

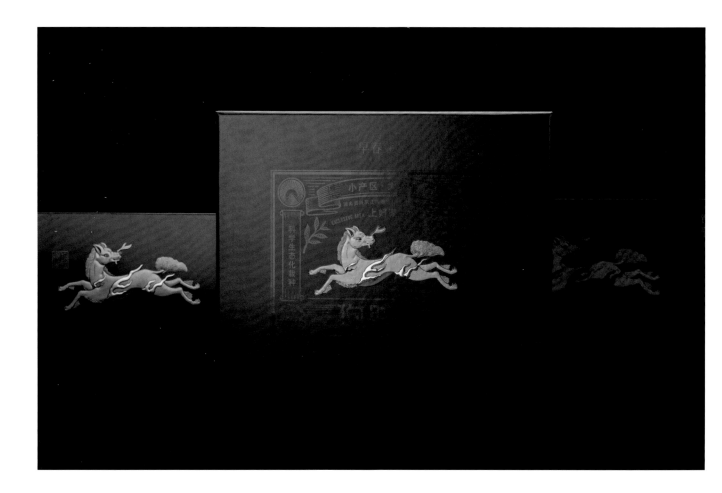

Xifeng Wine

Design: UNIDEA BANK   **Photography:** Chen Yue, Huang Renqiang

* Fenghuang, also known as phoenix, are mythological birds found in East Asian mythology that reign over all other birds.

Xifeng Wine is native to Fengxiang where is the legendary gathering place for the phoenix. In the packaging design, the phoenix is selected as the main visual element, and the story of "building a nest and attracting phoenix to come" is elaborated in an elegant and simple illustration. Different from the complicated design expression in traditional wine packaging, this simple design expression can make the brand stand out in the same kind of products.

Qian Ba Fang

Design: Sun Shine

This work inspired from Guizhou's local architecture and regional scenic spots.

Qian Ba Fang concentrates on authentic cuisine in Guizhou. It blends in Guizhou's different regional scenic spots and delicate cuisine in poster design, giving the brand a strong local character. Logo graphic combines Guizhou's Jiaxiu Tower and Drum Tower, and integrates "Qian", "Ba", and "Fang" three letters into logo to enhance brand recognition, which is impressive.

Formosa Song Thinking

Design: Hong-Wun Lu

This work is inspired from Taiwan's ballads, and fuse in many elements include pipa, lantern, peony, etc.

Developed from the idea of "thinking" and based on the earlier Formosa ballads, this work presents people's spiritual feeling of each song by a series of visual design. Through visual image, it helps people to rethink the old days in Taiwan, China, how people entrust their feeling in song and life. Differ from the modern life, these are more original and pure.

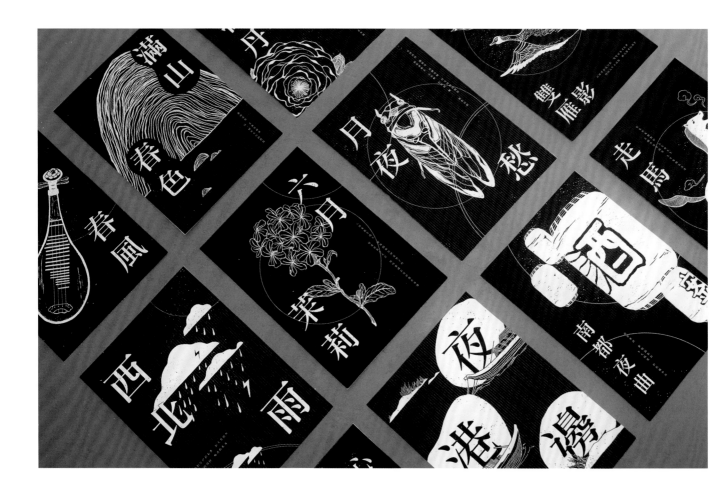

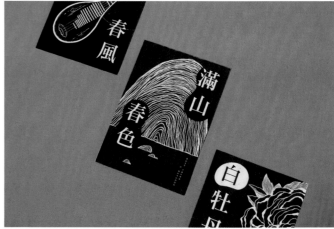

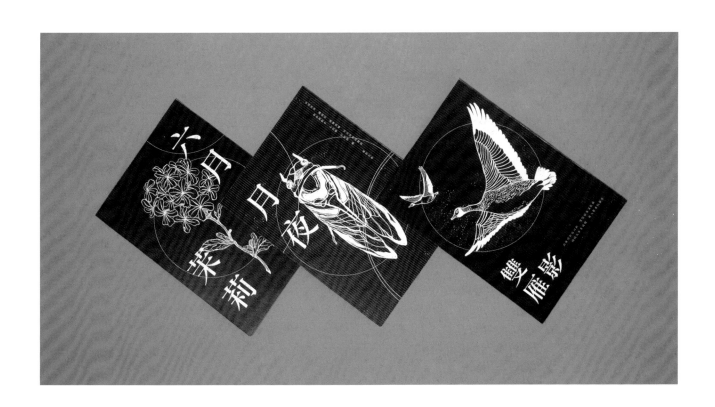

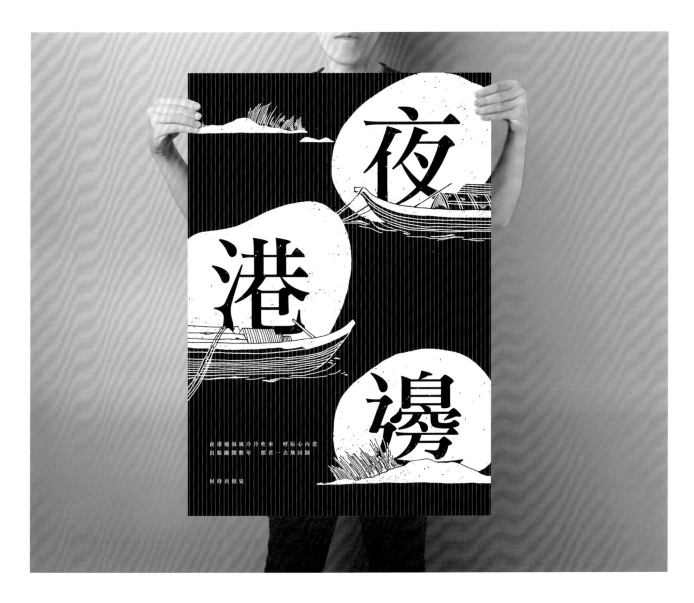

Karak Opera

Design: La Come Di

Emirati characters are the main subjects in this work.

The Karak Opera collection, designed from the Dubai based brand La Come Di, grasps on the Emirati culture, capturing unique love moments. It comes in a comic pop art style with a pinch of drama.

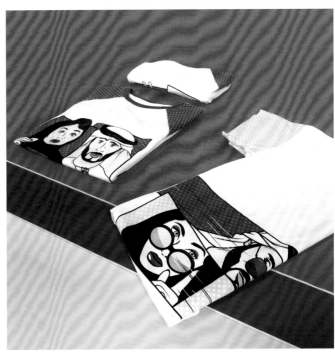

SKY TEA HOUSE

Design: MC BRAND

....

* Traditional Chinese patterns and architecture are the main characters in this work.

SKY TEA HOUSE regards quality as the core of the brand. Inspired by the vast amount of old shops, MC BRAND integrates classical Chinese patterns into logo, and takes the architectural appearance on lanes and alleys and the shape of old shop counter as illustrations and graphics. The application of purplish blue, retro beige and Chinese red strengthens the atmosphere of an old shop. Walk into SKY TEA HOUSE, there are full walls of tea cans, shopkeeper is weighing tea while other staffs are packaging them... These plentiful elements will provide the audience a five sense experience which will take them back to the time of old tea house.

Japan 2020

Design: Yusuke Yamazaki

....

** This work uses amount illustrations of Japanese landmark
buildings, classic figures, traditional mascot and many more.*

This is a Japanese cultural information program in preparation
for the Tokyo 2020 Olympic Games. It explains Japanese culture
intuitively in an easy-to-understand way, and also uses many
detailed illustrations that have strong visual effect.

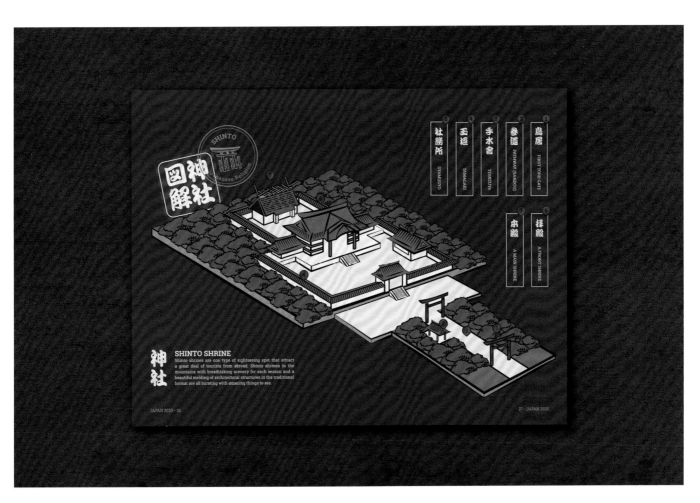

SHINTO SHRINE

Shinto shrines are one type of sightseeing spot that attract a great deal of tourists from abroad. Shinto shrines in the mountains with breathtaking scenery for each season and a beautiful melding of architectural structures in the traditional format are all bursting with amazing things to see.

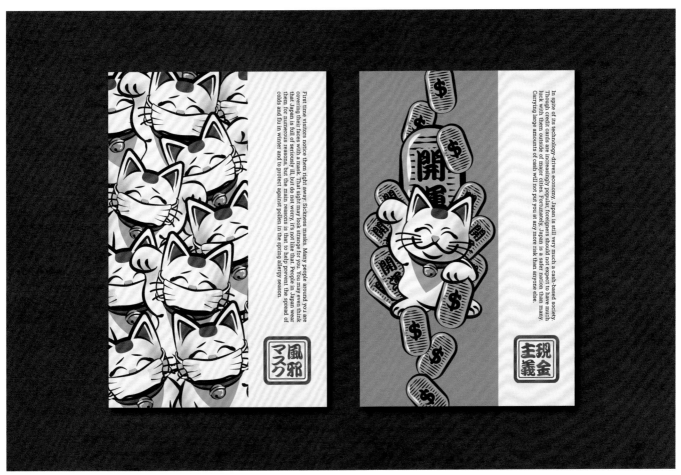

First time visitors notice them right away. Sickness masks. Many people around you are covering their faces with a mask. That sight may look strange for you. You may even think that Japan is full of seriously ill, but do not worry, it's not like that. People in Japan wear them for numerous reasons, but the main reasons is that to help prevent the spread of colds and flu in winter and to protect against pollen in the spring allergy season.

In spite of its technology-driven economy, Japan is still very much a cash-based society. Though credit cards are increasingly popular, foreigners should not expect to have much luck with them outside of major cities. Fortunately, Japan is a safer nation than many. Carrying large amounts of cash will not put you at any more risk than anyone else.

In Japan, it's customary to bathe in Onsen (hot spring), and this is almost always done in your birthday suit. It may be embarrassing at the beginning, but when you actually enter there, you will find that nobody cares about your figure. There is a phrase "hadaka no tsukiai" which means "naked communion" or "naked friendship" in Japan. Race, social class, academic background or anything doesn't even matter in there. If we get naked we are all equal.

Japan is a country with high standards of hygiene. You will notice its cleanliness by looking at the streets or public washrooms with no garbage. And you will be perplexed noticing the fact that there are not many garbage cans set up around Japanese cities. So where does the garbage go? The answer is simple. Most Japanese people will take their rubbish home or workplace with them rather than dispose of it when out and about.

Drinking in public places is not prohibited in Japan. You can even buy alcoholic beverages at convenience stores easily, but it does not mean that you can drink anywhere at any time. The reason that drinking in public is not a big problem in Japanese society is because its environment is built on individual morals and manner. Let's enjoy it with moderation without forgetting its cultural background.

Ramen is a noodle dish representative of Japan now, but in Japan there is a culture to slurp noodles. At first it might sound dirty, but actually this is a habit to enjoy more flavor. It is the same concept as wine connoisseurs gurgle wine, sucking air through their mouths to force air into the nasal passage, allowing the flavors to spread. However, there are a lot of people who do not slurp noodles even in Japan, and you also do not necessary have to do that, but why not? You are in Japan. Let's just give it a shot!

Tet Gift Box 2018

Design: Dong Hoa Concept

....

* Coin represents wealthy, while number "8" symbolizes the year of 2018 and the eternity infinity. Patterns are inspired by the motifs in the imperial palace.

Lunar New Year is one of the biggest festivals of the year. Vietnamese celebrate New Year with exciting activities. In order to convey the concept of "eternal flourishing", Dong Hoa Concept designed a simple, easy-to-use, both modern and classical Vietnamese packaging product.

Design: Dong Hoa Concept

Shimen Taste

Design: ROYU Brand Design

....

* Shijiazhuang is the capital and largest city of North China's Hebei Province.

This brand wants to restore the life in 1980s. By adding more traditional elements, audience can sense the magic of the old days' Shimen taste—sunlight shines on the old lane, nursery rhymes are singing, delicious food is everywhere... Shimen Taste aims for bringing the original flavor back to people.

Taoism's 28 Constellations' Image Creative

Design: Zhang Haocheng

* The 28 Mansions are part of the Chinese constellations system. They can be considered as the equivalent to the zodiacal constellations in Western astronomy, though the 28 Mansions reflect the movement of the Moon through a sidereal month rather than the Sun in a tropical year.

Based on the study of 28 constellations, designer uses symbolic image to create the work. He makes the symbols, vision and words interact with each other. And the symbols are also the manifestation of shape, color, space, image, and rule. He pays attention to the unique image of each star, and establishes an orderly system. Designer extracts specific symbol for each star, so that the characteristic of the star can be fully applied in the design.

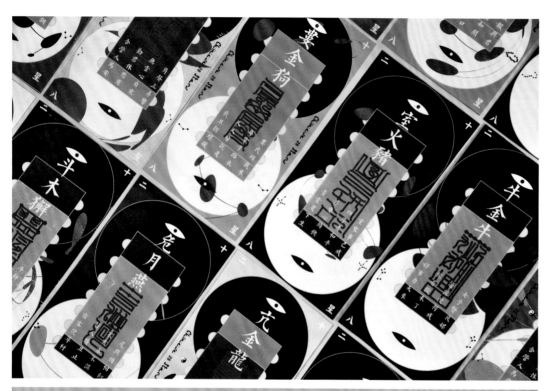

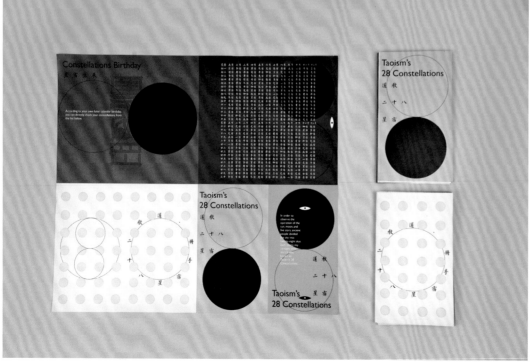

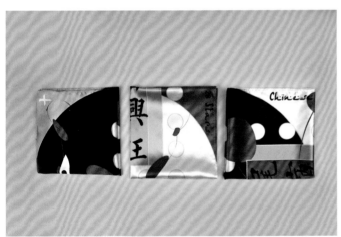

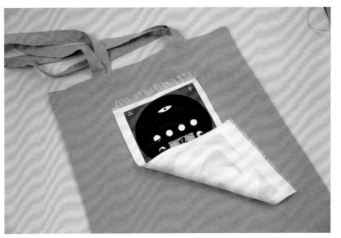

Wu Yi Rui Fang Tea Packaging

Design: ONE & ONE DESIGN

*** This work is inspired from the font design during the Republican period, and also gain inspiration from Chinese traditional tea cans.**

Rui Fang Tea is established by famous artist, Jiang Taiyuan in 1899. It was a famous tea house during the late Qing Dynasty. Rui Fang opened lots of branches in its golden age, which can be traced in its old cans, account books and bills. According to the shape of Rui Fang's cans, ONE & ONE DESIGN mix it with the font of the Republican period to create the packaging. It reflects the history of the brand and inherits its quality.

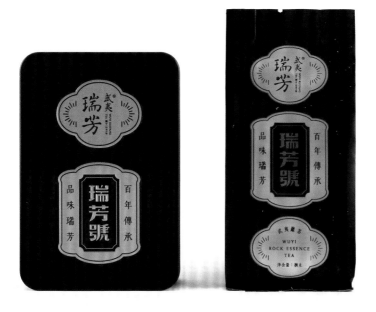

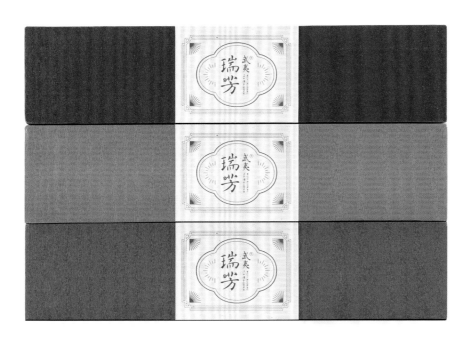

litchi > benefit

pineapple > thriving

persimmon > good thing

fish > surplus

sheep > lucky

bat > good fortune

Pu'er Caky Tea

Design: Huang Yufang
Client: Sung Yun Cao Tang Tea Studio

....

* Design applies Chinese homophonic greetings, totems, and calligraphy.

Designers tried to transcend the traditional wrappings of caky tea by adding some modern elements but conserving Chinese traditional spirit. It was a design plan about Chinese homophonic greetings. By the original color of rice papers and moderate printings, they selected two colors, six Chinese greetings, coupled with meaningful totems and calligraphy. Vivid illustrations made Pu'er tea much more active and to get its own characteristics. In this way, tea was conferred more cultural values and became worth collecting.

Soo Zee 23

Design: The Creative Method

....

* Elements include traditional armor, ancient celebrity clothing, zodiac, eastern food, etc.

Soo Zee 23 is a traditional Taiwanese beef noodle soup brand. Soo Zee in Sichuanese is "number", and "23" represents the number of blended herbs and spices that used to create their famous broth. The Chinese characters for "eat" (吃) and "23" (二三) are also featured in the identity to reinforce the authenticity of their speciality cuisine.

The Creative Method was asked to bring the story of Soo Zee 23 to life with a name, logo, identity creation, graphics, apparel, menus, tableware, a website and packaging. Soo Zee becomes a character of many forms that represents the art of mixing 23 herbs and spices to create an authentic beef noodle soup that people won't forget.

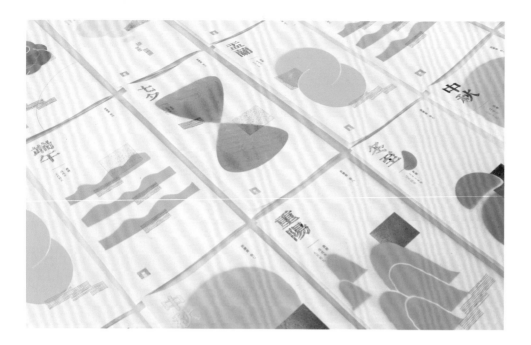

The Days of Joss Paper - Festipedia
Design: Fan Shuilun

* Joss paper are sheets of paper or papercrafts made into burnt offerings common in Chinese ancestral worship such as the veneration of the deceased family members and relatives on holidays and special occasions.

Nowadays, there are still many people have this habit, but they don't understand the content of joss paper since there are not many instruction manuals or explanations of joss paper provided in order to educate people about this culture when people buy it from funeral offerings store. In order to centralize the content, the book is comprised of 9 traditional festivals, so that readers will be able to understand more about the relationship between each festival and the joss paper through the texts and the pictures.

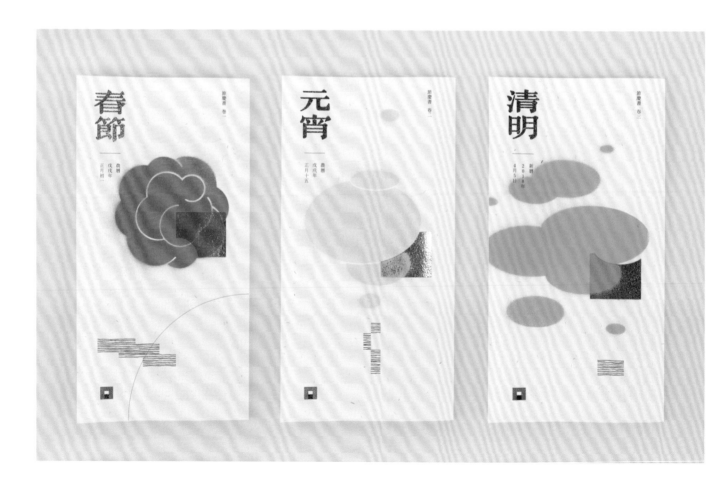

聖衣寶教學。

元寶

五四
長日
春月

七六
良貴
人馬

白色麗衣

八
個
貴
人

九
眼
貴
人

十
鴨
樣
寶
螺

十一
全
轉
送
詩
轉
進
坑

十二
上
邪
樣
容

十四
貴
人
合
柏
百

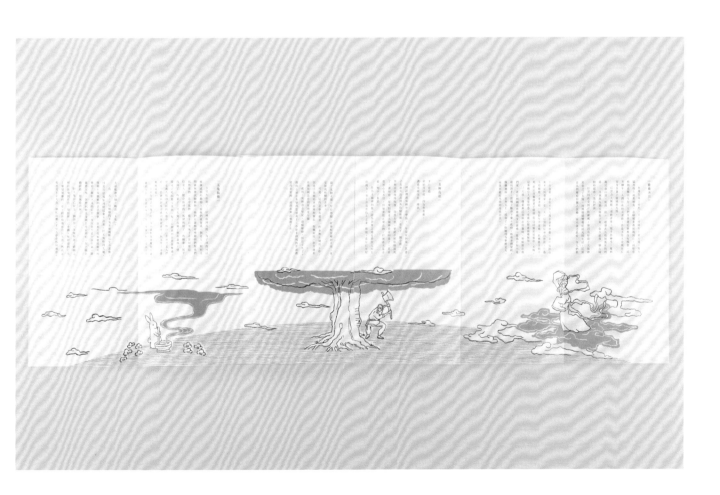

Hantabani

* This work embodies Japanese urban living fused with its underground vibes.

Design: Asthetíque Group

Hantabani encapsulates the tradition of Japanese cuisine with a distinctively tantalizing atmosphere that draws audience in through various elements: rare natural stones surfaces, patina metals, and lush fabrics surrounded. The general architectural lighting is dim and dramatic. Spotlights are featured on unique architecture, and art works inside would prompt people to photograph. Asthetíque created the Hantabani concept to create an exclusive, fun, and sophisticated atmosphere for an approachable price. Sublime experiences shouldn't be left for the wealthy and distinguished but for all to relish.

The Collective Series of Moon Cake Packaging Design

Design: Andon Design Daily Co.,Ltd.
Photography: Oat Yossaundharakul, Parinya Kawsrito

* Design elements include crane, peony, lotus, longevity peaches, dragon, palace maid, and many more.

Each package of the moon cake series was designed to be distinctly various, fun and trendy. The only design condition was that all packages needed to be propitious due to the belief that the moon cake is an auspicious pastry of the Mid-Autumn Festival.

Chinese New Year

Design: Lu Qifang

According to Chinese mythology, Nian is a beast that lives under the sea or in the mountains. Once every year at the beginning of Chinese New Year, the Nian comes out of hiding to feed. He would eat the crops and sometimes the villagers. The weaknesses of the Nian are purported to be a sensitivity to loud noises, fire, and a fear of the color red.

2018 is the year of the Dog in China. New Year's Eve is the most important festival in China. On this day, the whole family gathered to dining and set off firecrackers to scare away the monster called "Nian". Dogs are the most intimate partners of human beings, so they will guard the homelands and bring people with joy.

GDC Show in Xi'an

Design: Hills Culture Communication

....

* Elements applied in this work include: dragons, phoenix and magpie.

GDC Show is one of the most influential and professional design awards in China. The purpose of this activity is to reflect the current situation of the design industry in China, to conduct communication, and to pay attention to the current situation and future from a multi-dimensional perspective. It builds a free and interactive knowledge sharing platform for each participant, help them to refresh and deepen the value of graphic design and inspire the trend of design.

Nian Zai Yi Qi

Design: YOULIYOUJIE™

....

* The gift box is inspired by the Spring Festival market. Through the classic scroll paintings, it connects the old days and modern life together.

Nian Zai Yi Qi contains 3 sections: "Ji Huan Xi" New Year couplets set—blends into a variety of traditional elements to present a lively festive market; "Qi Huan Qing" New Year's red packet—on basis of New Year's dinner, designers put "He Huan dinner", "Tu Su wine" and "Ji Xiang fruit" along with lion dance, firecrackers and theater to create the series; "Ju Huan Yan" festive board game set—a game that can unite whole family to enjoy the fun.

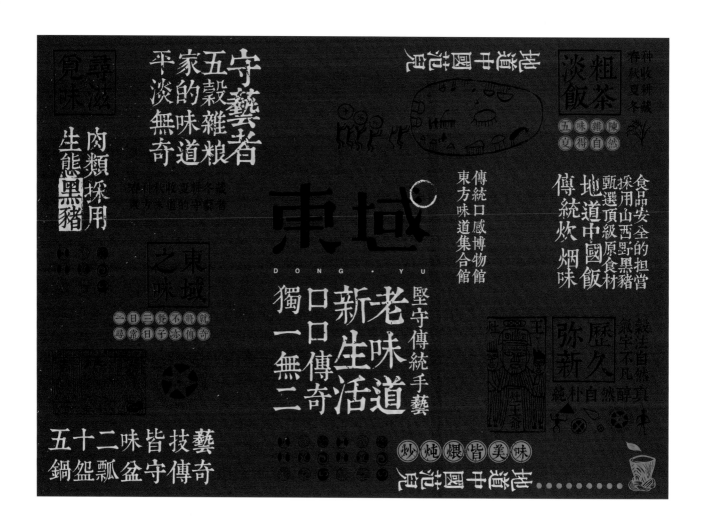

East Side

Design: Xu Rui

....

* In Chinese folk religion, Chinese mythology and Taoism, the Kitchen God also known as the Stove God, named Zao Jun, Zao Shen, or Zhang Lang, is the most important of a plethora of Chinese domestic gods that protect the hearth and family.

East Side takes emotion as its core marketing point. The brand creates an image of the Kitchen God. Both online and offline promotion are carried out in the tone of the Kitchen God, which adds more mystery, and also closes the distance with consumers. Red, black and yellow are the standard colors of the brand. Mysterious symbols and auxiliary graphics create a strong Chinese flavor to enhance the sense of brand recognition.

The Chic Formosa

Design: Mengchia Hu

* Daily scenery in Taiwan, China, plays a fundamental role in the design.

Taiwan, a beautiful island surrounded by oceans with four distinct seasons, was given the name "Formosa". Taiwan once had its time of prosperity and had gone through different stages of cultural baptism. However, the uniqueness of Taiwanese culture gradually faded away with the change of time. It's like amnesia, people no longer remember the beauty of this special island. This work aims to remind people how beautiful Taiwan is.

Tea Horse Flower Street

Design: YINGSHI & FASHENG

* Tea Horse Road was a tea trade route. It is also sometimes referred to as the Southern Silk Road or Southwest Silk Road, and it is part of a complex routes system connecting China and South Asia. This work presents Yunnan's Tea Horse culture.

"Tea Horse Flower Street" is a special experience block which built by Kunming, Yunnan province. It integrates Yunnan delicacies, folk snacks, handmade works, new literary creation, Baile Theater and theme bar.

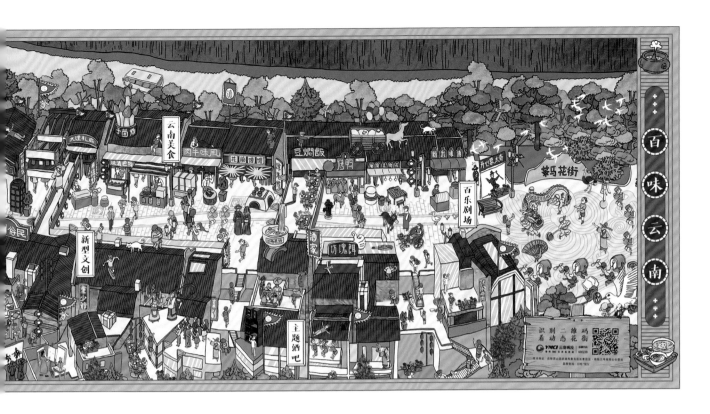

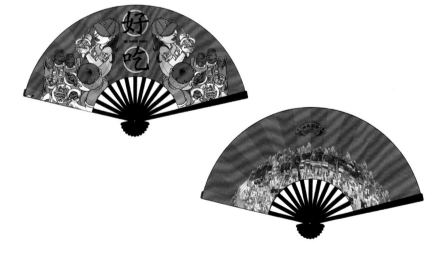

Chu Dai

Design: BEE DESIGN

....

* Matcha is finely ground powder of specially grown and processed green tea leaves. The powdered form of matcha is consumed differently from tea leaves or tea bags, and is suspended in a liquid, typically water or milk. Japan ranks No.1 in contemporary matcha industry.

"Chu Dai" means the first generation. This brand has two original intentions on doing business in China: Let matcha return to its birthplace (Chang'an); stick to the original quality. The purpose of brand upgrading is to direct reflect the first generation. While upgrading the brand, it has created a unique cultural aesthetic system. It integrates contemporary harmony and historical Tang style to convey the spirit of the brand.

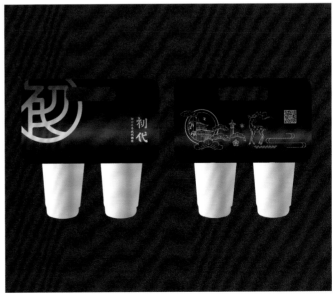

The Golden Silk Road

Design: TOMSHI AND ASSOCIATES

....

* The Silk Road was an ancient network of trade routes that connected the East and West. It was central to cultural interaction between the regions for many centuries.

Desert and Danxia landform record the pulsation of the earth. The Silk Road connects people and their spiritual belongings, and the Heart Sutra is the result in this background. This is the way that people yearn for conversion. It is also the natural traces of time polishing.

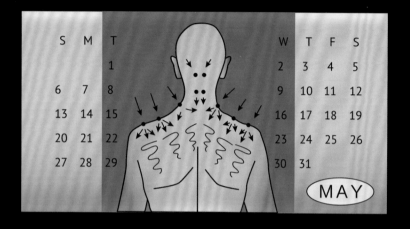

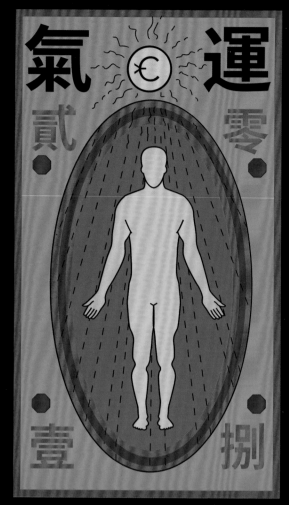

2018 Internal Alchemy Calendar

Design: Can Yang

* Taoism is a religious or philosophical tradition of Chinese origin which emphasizes living in harmony with the Tao. The Tao is a fundamental idea in most Chinese philosophical schools; in Taoism, however, it denotes the principle that is the source, pattern and substance of everything that exists.

The design of calendar was born from the curiosity to try and redeem Taoism Internal Alchemy and to look at them from a perspective devoid of cultural impositions and appreciate its social and historical content. The "old" world of superstitious associations, full of danger, unscrupulous behavior and irrational fervor, is now believed to be as coherent a sphere as the "new" arena of citizenship and faith in the daily life. These impulses, needs, and yearnings behind the redemptive society should be tied as they are to older cosmologies uniting the cosmos, the community, and the body. Expanding the space of religion remains the best way to channel the impulse for transcendence.

Degree Project

Design: Can Yang

....

* This project is a multi-dimensional study of "hidden" traditional Chinese culture and projection of contemporary Chinese modernity.

Designer combined quotations from taboo, folklore and commerce, and sought to root out the stubborn obstacles that traditional culture posed to achieving economic development. The adoption of the term "modernity" here signals a more sober, reflective, and critical stance that seeks to highlight a global snapshot between kitsch and apocalypse.

Oh Oh Pressure Go

Design: National Taichung University of Science and Technology
Team: Ku Pei-Wen, Chiou Yu-Ching, Shih Mei-Ju, Weng Ching-Te, Yang Po-Zhi
Photography: Yang Chinyao

Jiangshi, also known as Chinese "hopping" vampire/zombie, is a type of reanimated corpse in Chinese legends and folklore.

This design uses the Chinese spells and charms as main scheme. Designers describe ten psychological stresses as viruses that can make people infected and become zombies. They use a visual combination of intense colors. The heart symbolizes stresses that born from heart. This book is uses Chinese binding for one of its packaging, users can relieve their stress by having interaction while browsing the book. Another package uses a zombie cap as a model, along with a removable patch to help relieve the stress.

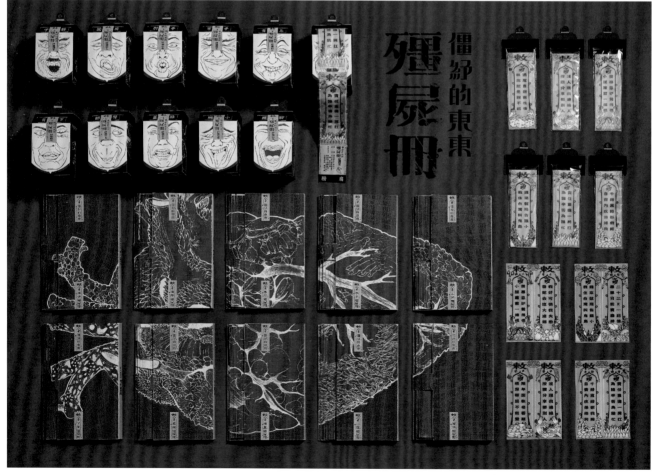

The Dunhuang Impression

Design: TOMSHI AND ASSOCIATES

* Dunhuang is a county-level city in northwestern Gansu Province, Western China. It was a major stop on the ancient Silk Road and is best known for the nearby Mogao Caves. It has also been known at times as Shazhou and, in Uyghur, Dukhan.

Dunhuang frescoes are more beautiful after years. The Dunhuang Impression returns to traditional culture, but intends to abstract Dunhuang Buddha statues and scenery by using the impressionic techniques. With a golden touch, the impression is re-colored, and the tradition is instantly renewed.

117

人生何處不尷尬

"好間界"系列產品設計

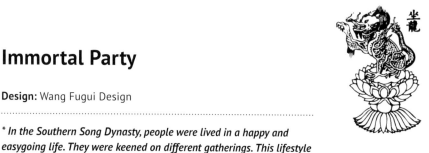

Immortal Party

Design: Wang Fugui Design

* In the Southern Song Dynasty, people were lived in a happy and easygoing life. They were keened on different gatherings. This lifestyle was so cozy that people felt like living in an immortal world, so they called it "immortal party".

People are always eager for finding out the secret and mystery beyond our living world. They trust in faith that everything is good to make their lives better. According to this, designer has read lots of materials and kept discovering the relationship between life and death. He obtained the prototype from ancient patterns, and sketched them in a more sophisticated way. This work is about to discover the Chinese traditional culture.

Lan Fong Yuen

Design: ABCDESIGN

....

* During the 50's Hong Kong, designers were good at mix the western elements with local culture, and create a simple visual style. This work is using classic design style from that time.

Lan Fong Yuen is a famous Hong Kong traditional restaurant serves traditional foods and drinks since 1952. ABCDESIGN was invited to redesign its visual identity including the graphic system applied on the interior decor and packaging. They modernized the visual identity while keeping the traditional flavor by using classic design style from 50's Hong Kong.

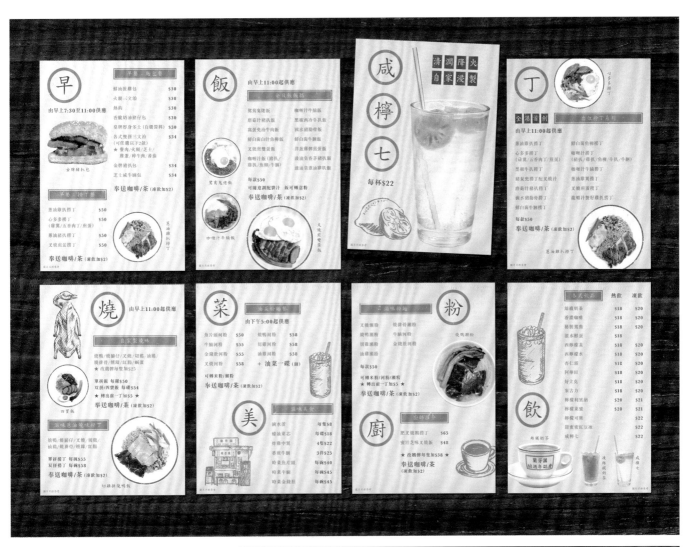

121

Chinese Shadow Puppet New Year Gift Set

Design: TOMSHI AND ASSOCIATES

....

* Shadow play, also known as shadow puppetry, is an ancient form of storytelling and entertainment which uses flat articulated cut-out figures (shadow puppets) which are held between a source of light and a translucent screen or scrim.

As a kind of Chinese folk culture, shadow puppet performance has been long out of people's everyday life and left a quite obsolete impression. TOMSHI AND ASSOCIATES took the responsibility and renewed the visual image of the folk culture. They reinvented the visual language of this traditional culture and celebrate new year with this gifts.

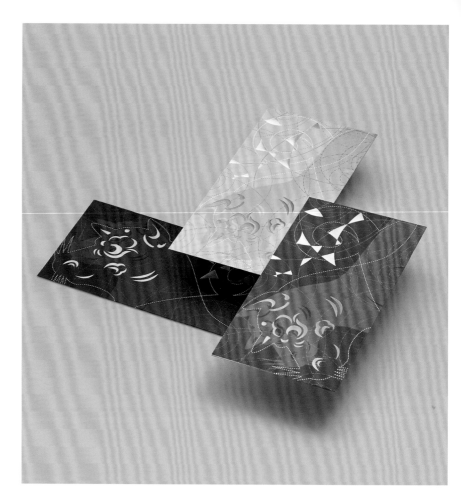

轉運風車

Hatagoya Rihei

Design: SAFARI inc.

....

* Edomoji are Japanese lettering styles, which were invented for advertising in the Edo period. The main styles of Edomoji include Kakuji, Kanteiryū, Yosemoji, Kagomoji, Higemoji, and Chōchinmoji.

The logo design for the Japanese sweet shop uses the bulky and rectangular Kakuji lettering style, which was invented for advertising and making seals in the Edo era. SAFARI appropriates the four letters from the shop's name into the image of Kakuji.

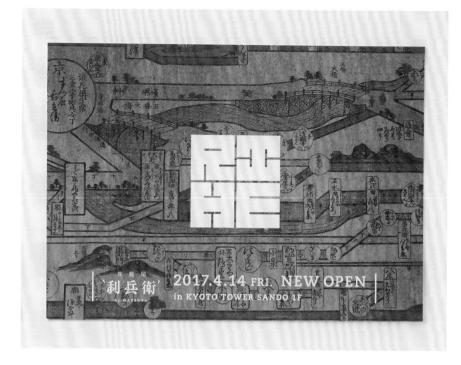

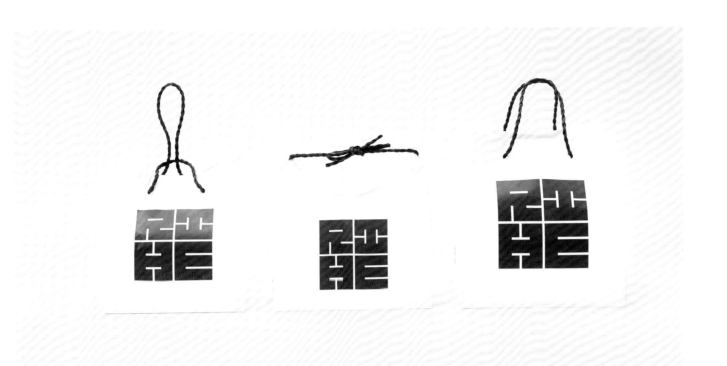

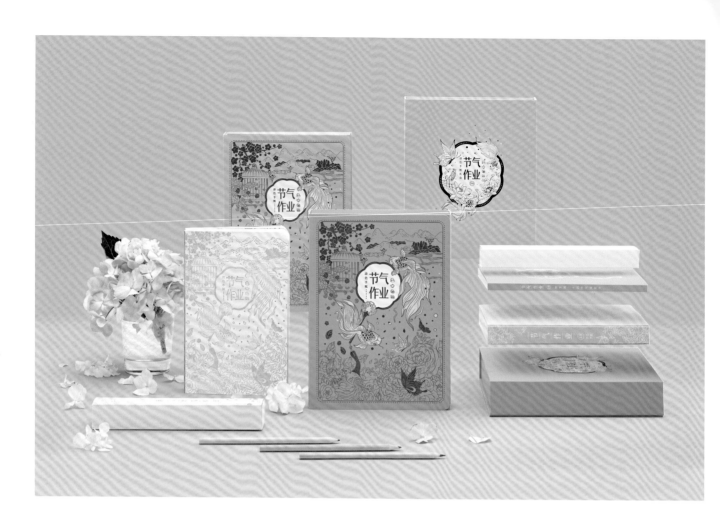

Solar Term
Painting Diary

Design: YOULIYOUJIE™

....

* A solar term is any of 24 points in traditional
East Asian lunisolar calendars that matches a
particular astronomical event or signifies some
natural phenomenon.

Solar Term Painting Diary is a color filling
book. YOULIYOUJIE™ designs this book
base on 24 solar terms. Through beautiful
illustrations, simple words, and delicate
cards, it shows us the scenery of life on
these days. This book serves as a companion
in Chinese people's life which to help them
reduce pressure, and also a guide book for
people to comprehend some common sense.

Shi Feng Shiang Pastry

Design: 2TIGERS design studio
Photography: Wang Ping

....

* Visual elements that used in this work include: cottonrose hibiscus and osmanthus, originates from a Chinese auspicious painting-Fu Rong Qi Gui, means a wealthy couple lives a flourishing life; rope and knot, they mean promises and also used as records of important events; magpie, symbolizes good luck and blessings; red cord and blessing couplet are about to bring a sense of Chinese tradition.

Shi Feng Shiang Taiwan Pastry, which is located on Shalu District in Taichung City, was founded over 30 years ago. Inheriting and promoting Taiwan pastry, which is part of Taiwanese culture as well as linking the decreasing hospitality to this generation. The principal who is the second-generation owner has opened the second-generation store of Shi Feng Shiang in downtown. With a profound cultural background, Taiwan pastry and innovative small cake that pass down the tradition are the cores of the second-generation store of Shi Feng Shiang to reach a balance between tradition and innovation.

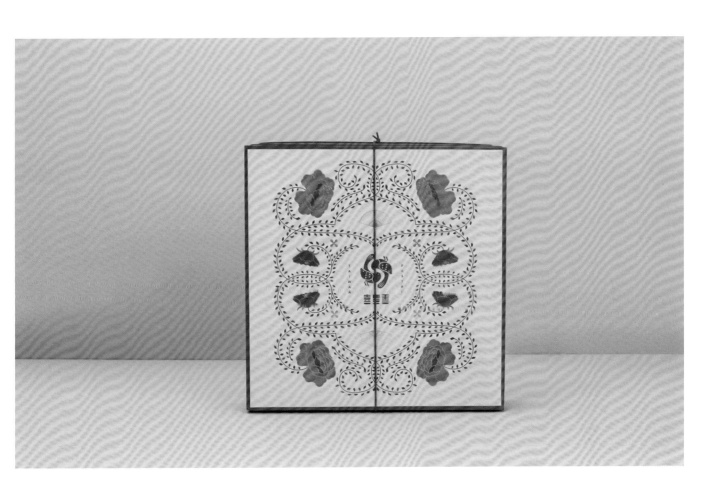

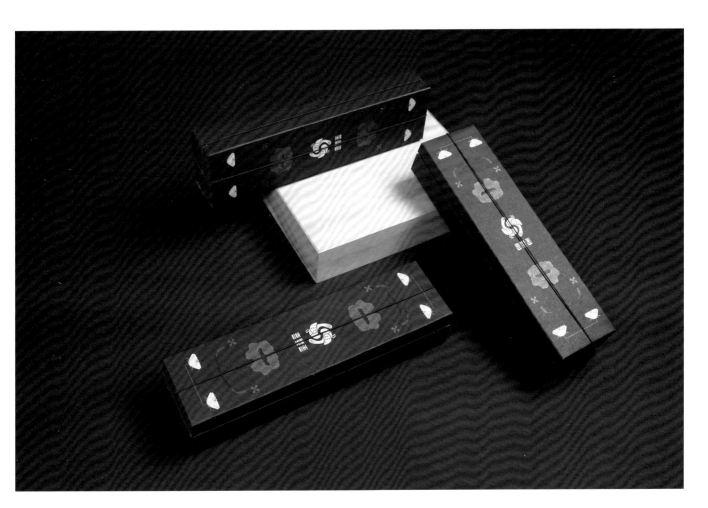

Chong Kio Farmacia Chinesa Co.

Design: 2TIGERS design studio
Photography: Pai Weichi

* Inspired by the philosophy of "roundness and mean", the main visual of "circle within square and bisection" is developed; furthermore, the concept of sincerity, earnestness and everlasting vivacity is combined with traditional heritage to give birth to the brand of Chong Kio.

Chong Kio Farmacia Chinesa Co. was founded in Macau in 1950. Due to the historical background at that time, Chinese expatriates from all over the world were faced daunting challenges of returning to their hometown. In order to evoke the feeling of missing home, the letter "C" is used on the brand logo as a symbol of "home". This brand aspires to promote traditional Chinese medicine and healthcare. Its "Old Brand Rejuvenation" strategy also retains the virtues and wisdom of ancestors. It perfectly fuses with novel, pink color, and traditional Chinese red color.

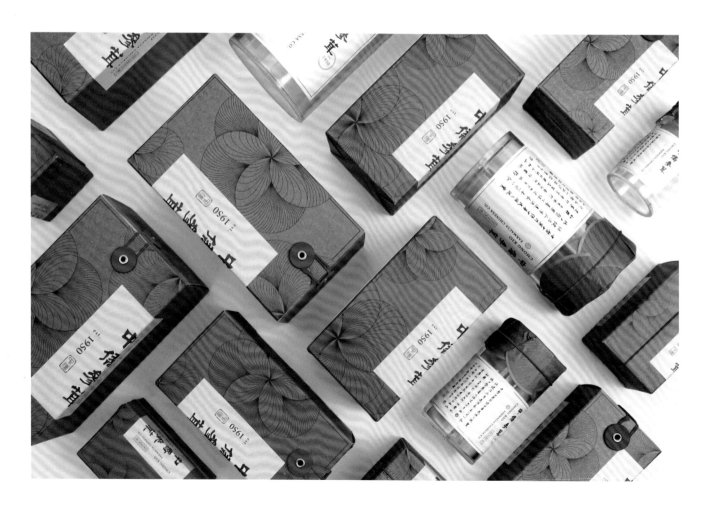

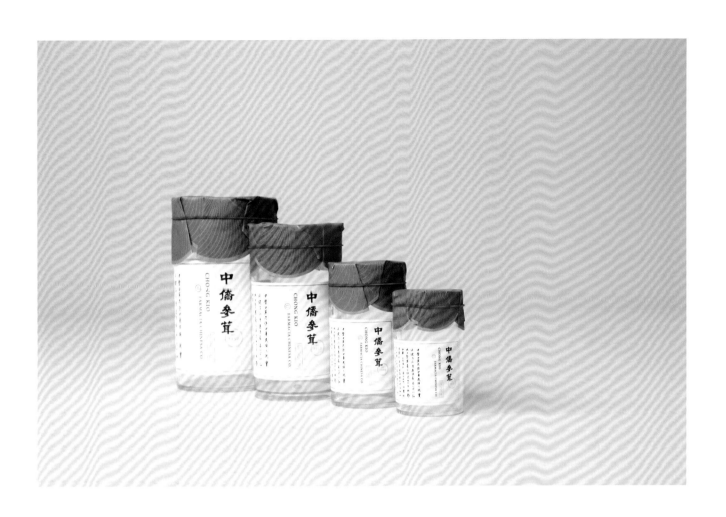

Rui He Tea Pu'er - Five Elements in Buddhism

Design: SanYe Design Associates

....

* This work implants with the five elements in Indian Buddhism, earth, water, fire, wind and space, respectively symbolizing perseverance, stability, warmth, fluidity and catholic mind.

In order to appear the distinction of product categories, designers applied the five elements in Indian Buddhism: earth, water, fire, wind and space. They are also presented as different producing areas of tea and their representative properties.

The trademark is converted into the form of paper-cutting window and combined with the five elemental images to present the elegance originated from the eastern world. It enables the givers to pass on their feelings with blessed wishes to the recipients. The disposal of color, white and gold, respectively indicates humility and refinement. The upper and lower lids of the package is designed with simple structure which makes the product be able to be spread out and placed flatly before molding and convenient for transportation and storage operation. The division design of the inner box can be transformed into different forms according to the content and quantity of the product to meet the needs of the four forms of transportation.

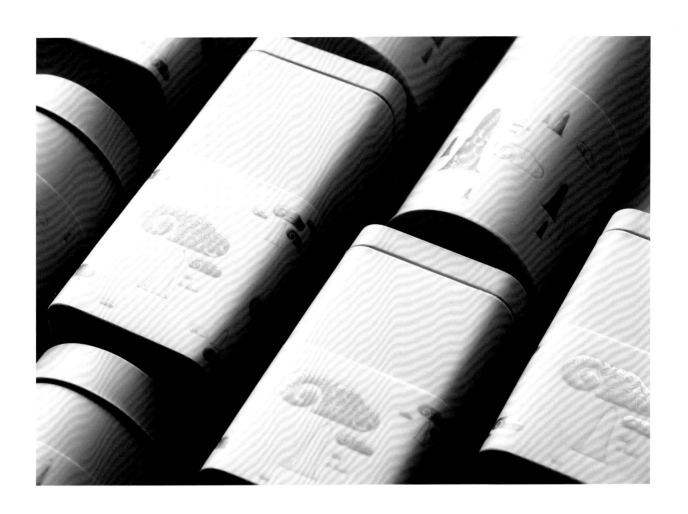

Lu Mei Institute

Agency: Asia Chimian Company   **Design:** Amiao   **Photography:** KM

* Braising is a combination-cooking method that uses both wet and dry heats. It is also used extensively in the cuisines of Asia, particularly Chinese cuisine and Vietnamese cuisine, where soy sauce is often the braising liquid.

Lu Mei Institute is the first agency that focus on making braised food. This brand extracts the concept of "institute", along with data, research, experiment, sheet, icon, and black and red colors, it forms a professional dining "institute". There are also many interesting materials like text, symbol, and method.

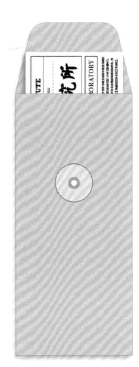

Ninigi

Design: Estudio Yeyé
Photography: Estudio Yeyé

....

** In Japanese mythology, Ninigi (ニニギ) was
the son of Ame no Oshihomimi, and grandson
of Amaterasu. He was sent to earth to plant
rice.*

Estudio Yeyé transformed this myth into a
branding project, and grew it into different
mediums such as packaging, furniture
design, object design, multimedia and
interior design, where they combined the
port feeling with Japanese spirituality
and Nó theater. The Nó is unique for
its slowness, its austere grace and its
distinctive use of masks. It truly represents a
specific feature of Japanese culture, which is
to find beauty within subtlety and formality.

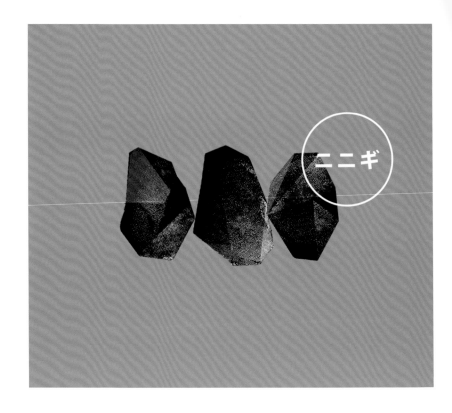

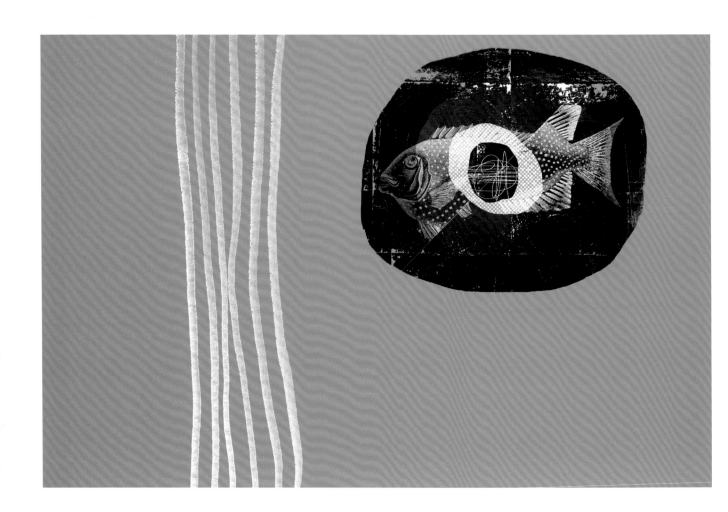

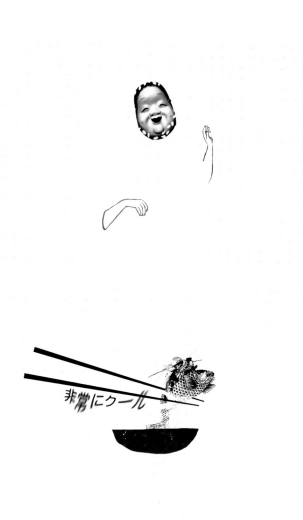

非常にクール

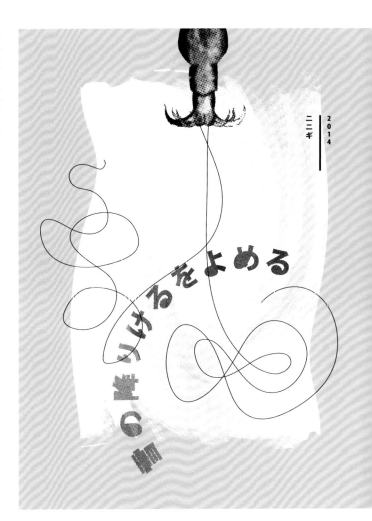

ニニギ
2014

闇の葉より来るをよめる

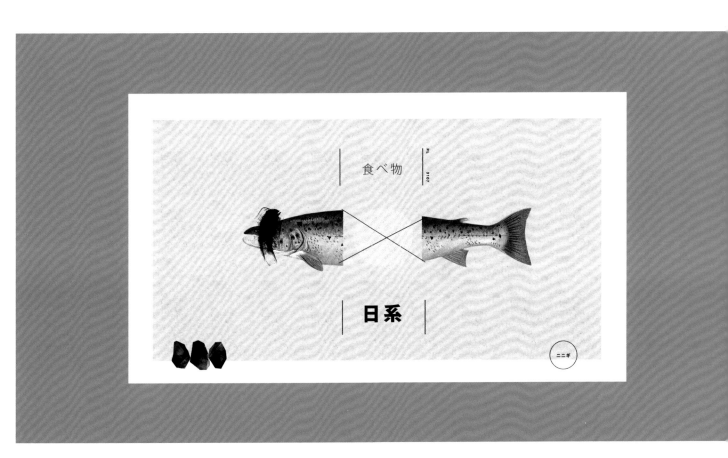

食べ物

PL 3107

日系

ニニギ

Journey Oriental Kitchen & Bar

Design: Thinking*Room

....

* Journey to the West is a Chinese novel published in the 16th century during the Ming Dynasty. It is one of the Four Great Classical Novels of Chinese literature. The novel is an extended account of the legendary pilgrimage of the Tang Dynasty Buddhist monk Xuanzang who traveled to the "Western Regions", that is, Central Asia and India, to obtain Buddhist sacred texts and returned after many trials and much suffering.

Journey Oriental Kitchen & Bar is a contemporary Chinese restaurant & bar in Surabaya. A large selection of dim sum to tea bar are served in this place. The name, Journey, derived from one of the great classical novels of Chinese literature, *Journey to the West*. The "J" and "O" in the logotype is composed from Chinese letters for journey (程). Inspired with the original story, designers created a brand and concept that brings all four characters came alive, as The Monkey King and his friends have stopped by to the place while they travelling to the West. Four life-size sculptures holding kitchen utensils was also created to complement the ambience with some humor and wittiness.

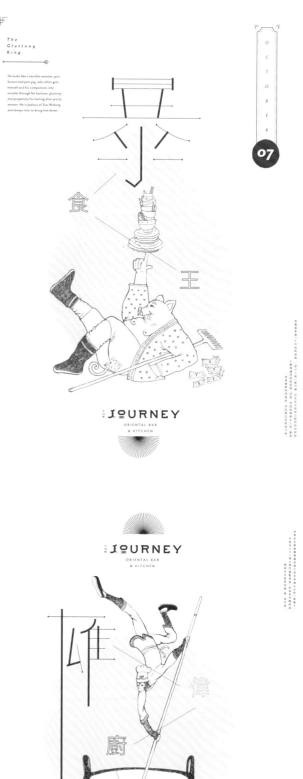

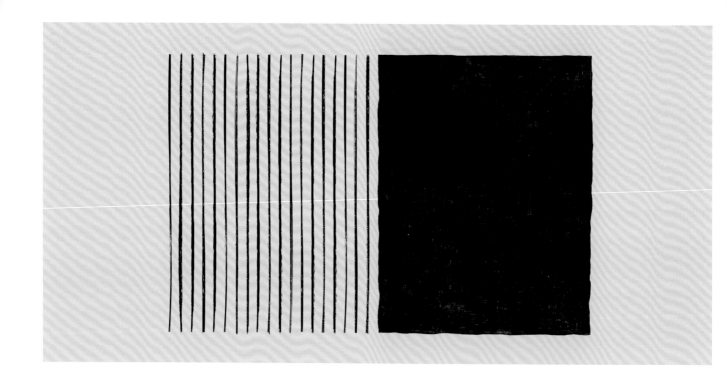

Acts Without Effort

Design: Yi-Hsuan Li

* In Chinese philosophy, yin and yang describes how seemingly opposite or contrary forces may actually be complementary, interconnected, and interdependent in the natural world, and how they may give rise to each other as they interrelate to one another.

Hsieh Ying-Chun is the architect who focuses on reconstructing buildings after natural disaster. Acts Without Effort presents Hsieh's practice of post-disaster reconstruction and his concepts. It displays yin and yang ("dark-bright"); one is long and uneven lines composed of continuous and repetitive drawings, the other half is large areas composed of ceaseless and overlapping sketches. The lines are outlined by the victims of earthquake which depict Hsieh's concept of "taking victims to build their homes with their own hands". The straight lines also exemplify the steel structure that Hsieh has been promoting. On the other hand, the color blocks made up of pencil lines represent lands and environment.

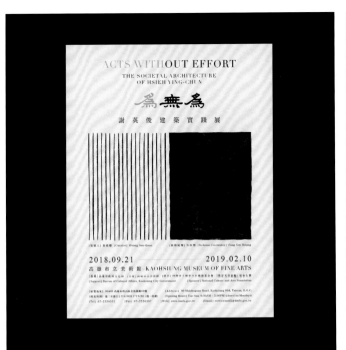

Detoxification

Design: Lilly Ark, Atcharani Thanabun, Jiang Pei-Xuan, Li Zi-Xuan, Xu Si-Ying, and Gao Li-Ting

* This project is inspired from traditional Chinese medicine.

Designers chose a kind of flower that is beautiful, but contained lethal toxicity. However, this kind of flower can be used as traditional Chinese medicines that have great benefits to human body. They divided those flowers into two different characteristics: cold and warm. Respectively, they collected them into two booklets and also wrote down the medicinal properties of toxic flowers, medicinal properties after turning it into materials and medicinal part. Designers picked some classic and contrast color to give prominence to the theme. They tried to use cans or glasses pack the medicine. Packing different kinds of medicine into different packages, patients are able to take the medicine due to their demands.

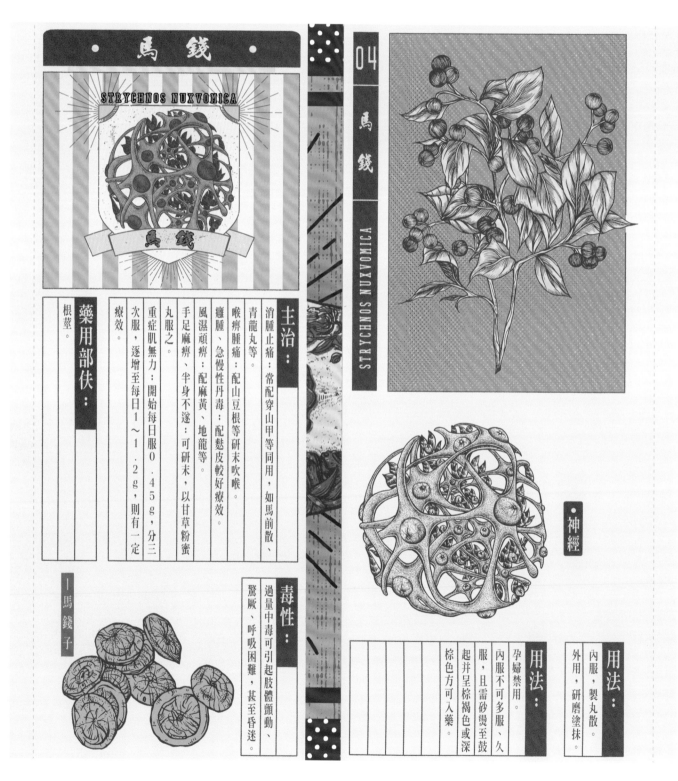

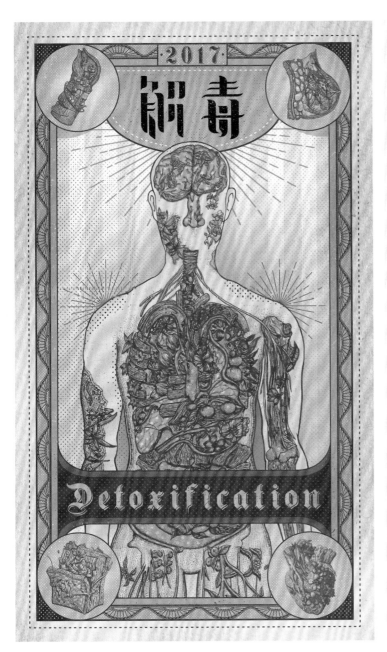

2017

解毒

Detoxification

第十首

·野棉花·

鼻疳：全草搗爛，以布包塞鼻

目翳：取之烤軟揉成團，在手腕上太淵穴放一有孔銅錢，藥敷錢上，布包紮，一至二小時取下。左翳貼右，右翳貼左。

瘰疾：與常山、黃豆共煮熟，去藥黃豆曬幹研成細粉酒調為丸、雄黃為衣，瘧前服十粒。

瘰疽不潰：取之水煎服。

腳氣病：與豬腳燉食。

發癢子：取之水煎服。

蜈蚣咬傷、口瘡：取之搗爛敷

蟲牙：取之含口內牙痛處。

— 解毒·藥簽 —

松潘烏頭

松潘烏頭

Aconitum sungpanense

松潘烏頭

Aconitun sungpanense

ACONITUM SUNGPANENSE

野棉花

URENA LOBATA L.

Mask Fruit Wine

Design: Zhang Xiaoning

....

* The Chinese opera is one of the oldest known dramatic art forms worldwide. Chinese opera masks are significant in a way that they represent the performers' or characters' personalities, intense moods, and status quo even.

Mask, in any civilization of the world, it's like a general language of emotions. In fact, there is more than one soul under the mask! The Mask Fruit Wine packaging is designed to balance the Chinese context with modern life. The mainstream customer groups are young women, therefore, the overall style is more simple and fresh.

Modern Medicine Co.

Design: Adrienne Hugh

* Design inspiration comes from traditional Chinese medicine packaging.

Modern Medicine Co. is a fabricated medicine company inspired by traditional Chinese medicine. Referencing the vibrant visual culture and history of Chinese medicine packaging found in Hong Kong, the design is a contemporary twist on traditional packaging. Meanwhile the contents of the medicine provide commentary on the various social and environmental "ailments" that plague those who live in Hong Kong.

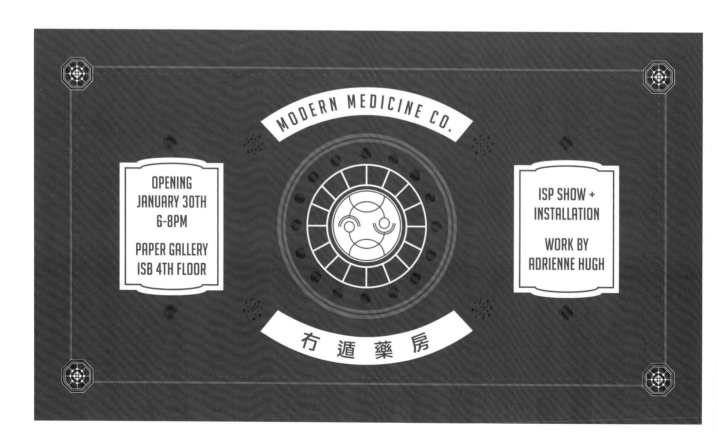

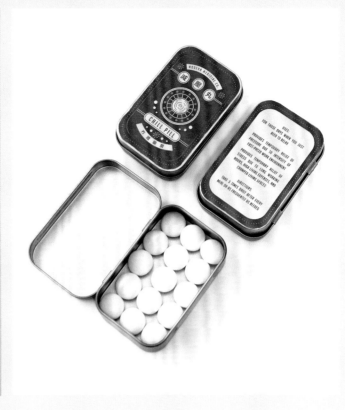

151

Out of The Box

Design: Yang Quanwen (TOOZ)

....

* Designer creates this work base on traditional Chinese cuisine.

The client is located in New Zealand. This design is to reflect the distinctive culture of traditional Chinese snacks from various aspects of life, like dough, mink, mix, basket, etc.

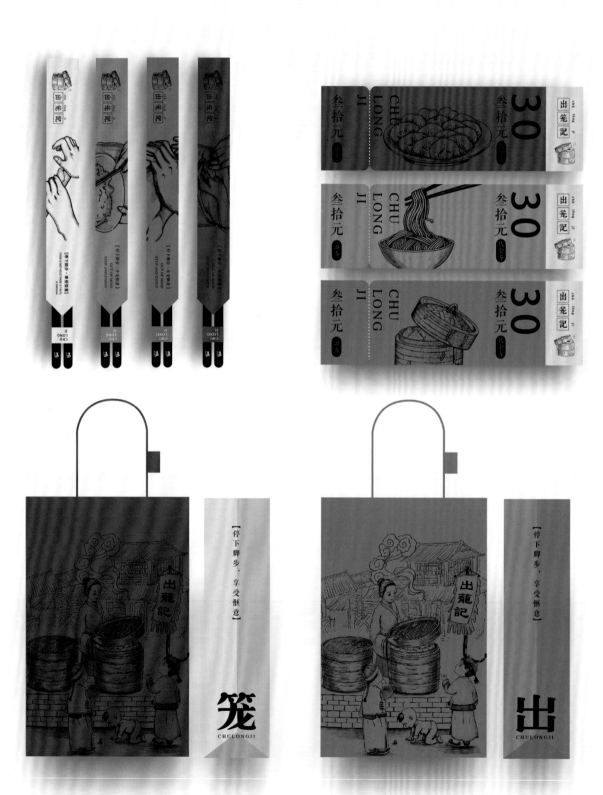

K11 Red Packet

Design: Pengguin

....

* Patterns in this design are inspired from Chinese folk adage.

With traditional New Year's patterns and bright colors, Pengguin creates a series of red packet with different meanings. For example, blossom means good fortune and richness are about to come; fish represents abundance; clouds symbolize promotion; fans on behalf of opportunities. Gold and silver are used to convey a concept of "new year with a new start".

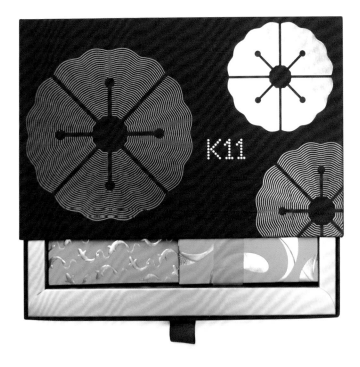

Kowloon Buffet Dim Sum & Hot Pot

Design: just-o studio

One thing that well represents Hong Kong's traditional and contemporary culture is the red lantern, which can be easily spotted on the street of Hong Kong.

Kowloon Restaurant is a Hong Kong buffet Dim Sum & hot pot restaurant in Hanoi, Vietnam. Kowloon opened its door in 2016, and quickly became popular among young food-lovers, especially Dim Sum lovers, because of its authentic Hong Kong cuisines and a very affordable price. The new identity needs to have authentic Hong Kong feeling when people first see it, so designers have looked into "what makes Hong Kong different"—the food, the culture, the signage on the street, etc.

Moon Cake Packaging Design

Design: XY Creative

....

* A moon cake is a Chinese bakery product traditionally eaten during the Mid-Autumn Festival. The festival is for lunar appreciation and moon watching, when moon cakes are regarded as an indispensable delicacy.

XY Creative has put forward three thoughts. The first is sharing: take the full moon as the theme and make family size moon cakes. Hence, people can gather around and share the pastries, which is match today's Chinese "catering rules". Second one is handmade art: to promote Chinese traditional handmade moon cake so that to express the difference between the South and the North cuisine culture and their integration today. Last one is the image of the moon: gain inspiration from poems and create a pure and beautiful package.

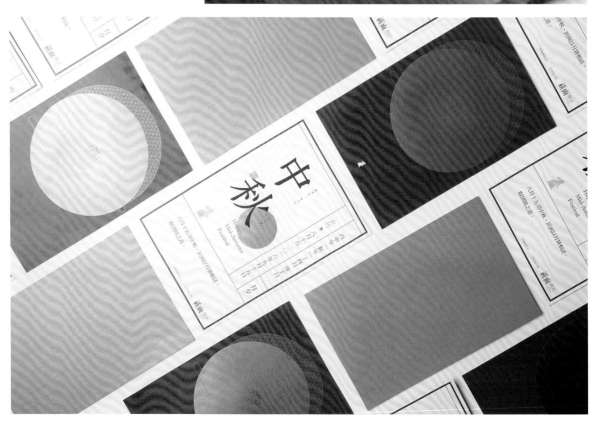

Sofitel Legend Metropole Hanoi Moon Cake Box

Design: Incamedia
Photography: Incamedia

. . . .

* Folk games and traditional Vietnamese handicraft product are applied in the design.

The Incamedia design team has collaborated with artist Thanh Phong to recreate the panorama of the traditional full moon night in August in the illustration. Folk games are chosen as the main idea. All the packaging design, textures, materials, gift items... are Incamedia creative impression of impressive traditional. The special feature of the Metropole moon cake box design this year is "Special Gift" which is a mask of paper—a traditional handicraft product of Vietnamese culture. This is really a surprise gift to take viewers back to the old days. Each design detail of the Metropole moon cake box is carefully calculated to bring pleasant surprise and not lose the elegance of the brand.

Little Tokyo Map

Design: KittoKatsu

* Traditional Japanese maneki-neko, sashimi, comic figures are well presented in the design.

Düsseldorfs buzzing center of Japanese cultural life with countless great restaurants, shops, bakeries and everything else the Japanophile is looking for. Designers have included all the go-to places as well as some personal recommendations of their favorite spots. They are happy to present the Little Tokyo Map.

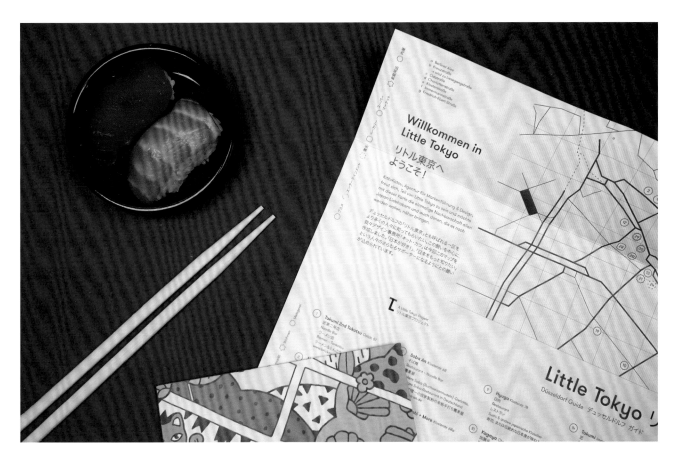

Lecture of Piety and Honest

Design: 9 × 9. Design

* Xiaolian, which is piety and honest, was the standard of nominating civil officers started by Emperor Wu of Han in 134 BC. In Confucian philosophy, it is a virtue of respect for one's parents and ancestors.

Lecture of Piety and Honest is a public welfare learning organization that promotes traditional Chinese learning. However, it is difficult to attract young people to join it. Therefore, designers use the way of designing a fashion brand to deduce traditional Chinese culture and use the new typesetting method to integrate Chinese and English, which makes the brand maintaining the traditional characteristic as well as holding the sense of fashion.

PostCare - Roosterious Year 2017

Design: i'll studio

....

* Chinese New Year, usually known as the Spring Festival, is an important Chinese festival celebrated at the turn of the traditional lunisolar Chinese calendar. Year 2017 is the year of the Rooster. The Rooster is the tenth of the 12-year cycle of animals which appear in the Chinese zodiac related to the Chinese calendar.

In the year of the Rooster, i'll studio presents to audience a carton of blessings from rooster legacy with postcards, angpows, stickers and planner. With the spirit of rooster, people will live towards a luxurious year on health, wealth and happiness.

Gift For Good 2017

Design: The Box Brand Design Ltd.   **Photography:** Ariom Leung

In Chinese and other East Asian and Southeast Asian societies, a red packet is a monetary gift which is given during holidays or special occasions.

New beginning, fresh starts, reaffirmations of love and promises for a brighter future all come to mind as people ring in a new year. The Box Brand Design Ltd. puts these desires into red packet and present to people the "Golden Flavor" and "Circle of Blessings". They wish to send inspirational greetings in new journey of good life.

Daxiang Tibetan Tea

Design: Guge dynasty

* Mani stones are stone plates, rocks and/ or pebbles, inscribed with the six syllabled mantra of Avalokiteshvara, as a form of prayer in Tibetan Buddhism.

The product packaging is based on the prototype of Mani stone, covering integral elements and manufactured by convex-concave craft. It completely presents the layer sense of carving. It makes the product simple yet rich gradation, and interprets the Tibetan culture precisely. It not only increases the impact and aesthetic feeling, but also strengthens the user's recognition.

Mount Huang Impression

Design: Langcer Lee

* Mount Huang, also known as Huangshan, is a mountain range in southern Anhui province in eastern China. The area is well known for its scenery, sunsets, peculiarly-shaped granite peaks, Huangshan pine trees, hot springs, winter snow, and views of the clouds from above.

The external packages of the two tea are hand-painted old streets of Anhui province and scenery of Mount Huang—"The Greeting Pine", "Flying Stone", and "Sea of Clouds". Designer also takes Hui-style architecture, Ma Tau Wall, as prototype and uses classic flip structure on packaging. The inner box depicts the changes of the old streets from ancient to the present in order to demonstrate the cultural accumulation.

LKY Tea

Design: The Box Brand Design Ltd.
Photography: Joey Lo

* Chinese ancient genre painting and Chinese idioms are well displayed in this work. For example, "San Yang Kai Tai" literally means three rams bringing bliss, it can also translate as "May you life be auspicious!"

Lam Kei Yuen Tea Co.,Ltd. has been running business for more than 60 years. To revamp and make difference to traditional brand, modern styles are applied to capture the essential concepts of the tea ceremony and brand character, which reflect the core value of the traditional tea brand.

Cha Tzu Tang Camellia Oil Gift Box   **Design:** Victor Branding Design Corp.

* The design of this product is inspired from traditional Taiwanese cha tzu oil.

Every aspect of the bottle design for Taiwan's Cha Tzu Tang Camellia Oil embraces the idea of "a drop of award-winning oil, rare and exquisite". From its shape, to the oil-drop nozzle and the handmade glass bottle, the whole design is conveying the highest quality of this product.

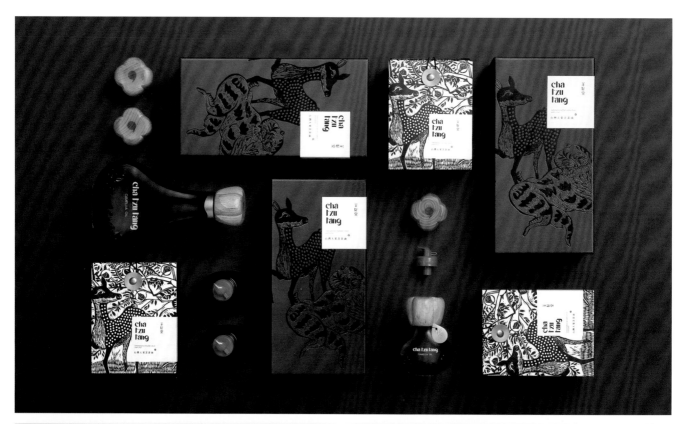

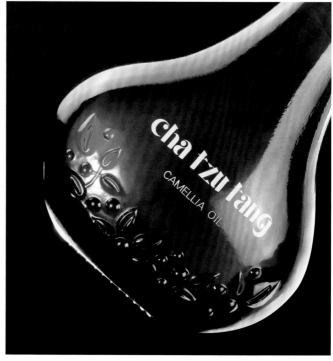

Moonzen Brewery Package Design

Design: Yosuke Ando

* The design is inspired from a Chinese treasure chest.

Six-pack beer packaging for Hong Kong based craft beer company Moonzen Brewery. The packaging resembles a Chinese treasure chest with six doors opening to six Moonzen gods. Decorative illustrations cover the surface of the package with references to beer along with traditional Chinese motifs, whilst the monotone box creates a contrast against the colorful label designs.

Oto

Design: Estudio Yeyé
Photography: Estudio Yeyé

* Katsushika Hokusai was a Japanese artist, ukiyo-e painter and printmaker of the Edo period. Born in Edo (now Tokyo), Hokusai is best known as author of the woodblock print series Thirty-six Views of Mount Fuji which includes the internationally iconic print, The Great Wave off Kanagawa.

Oto was inspired by Hokusai's Great Wave and ukyo-e painting. The painter goes deep on a spectacular process of observation to freeze a moment beyond the capabilities of human eye, capturing pure physics. Hokusai prints depict further aspects of fluid motion, as well as faithful representations of plants and animals. Designer took this principle to develop an exercise on light, to capture waves of movement that are hidden for the eye but revealed in nature's manipulation.

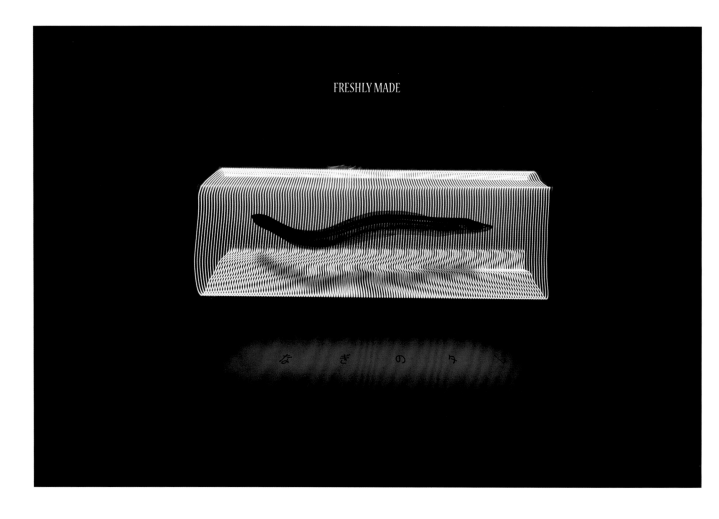

Maca Tea

Design: ROYU Brand Design

This work is inspired from ancient totem.

Maca Tea is a pure black tea. It uses the mysterious totem as element for promotion, showing the mysterious medicinal efficacy of Maca and a long history of planting.

YAU SIK SAN

Design: 1983ASIA

* "YAU SIK SAN" equal to "You've got the God of Cookery", which is a slang of Cantonese, means someone is a lucky gourmet with a great feast. The oriental astrology reads that the God of Cookery is symbolizes clothing, food, luck, and longevity. Embraced with mild disposition, exquisite behavior and elegant spirit, the God of Cookery, as a lucky gourmet, is good at cooking and is optimistic on the way of chasing happiness and joviality in life.

1983ASIA hopes that visual experience of the brand can demonstrate characteristics of Guangdong cuisines systematically. Since the Qin Dynasty, Guangdong has attracted immigrants from the central plains areas, whose cultural background is profound, so it is viewed as one of the birthplaces of Chinese civilization. Besides, thanks to its location at the shipping hub in the South China Sea, Guangdong has become the earliest birthplace of the Maritime Silk Road. Gradually, it has integrated into the formation of three major ethnic groups—Guangfu, Hakkas, and Chaoshan. 1983ASIA has incorporated these contents into the brand design, creating a jubilant and lively visual system.

Ubon

Design: Estudio Yeyé
Photography: Estudio Yeyé

....

* The brand was inspired by the landscapes of the Ubon region in Thailand, which is famous for their lotus flower culture and its beautiful Buddhist temples.

Ubon was born with the aim of bringing the true flavors of Thai food to the Middle East, focused on achieving a unique proposal through the authenticity of its dishes. This brand wants to present that tropical and millenary recipes that are distinguished from the typical food of Bangkok. The brand has a minimal black and white palette that is vitalized with small tones in purple, to give life to a bold and forceful graphic system.

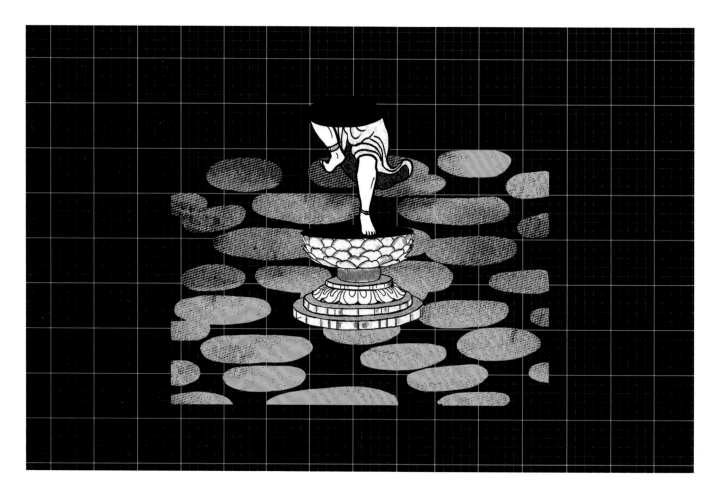

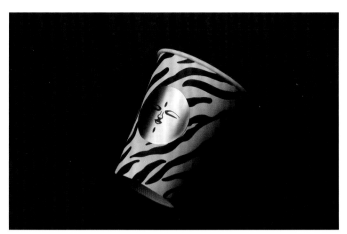

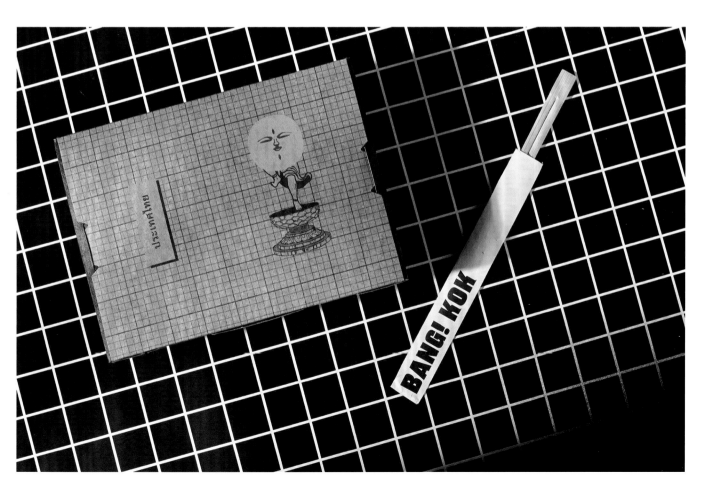

ZEN

Design: 1983ASIA

* In traditional Chinese residential decoration, "five-colored auspicious cloud" and "Ru Yi" are widely used because they represent people's warm blessings and aspiration.

Zen is a high-end Chinese style home furnishing brand. 1983ASIA have gathered traditional Chinese elements and made new analysis and studied on them before designing in an attempt to create a rare yet with new meaning brand. Considering the future development of the brand and different types of products, designers differentiate brand images in terms of material and color, and this may help to maximize the value of the brand.

Qinli Cake

Design: ROYU Brand Design

....

* Qinhuangdao is a port city on the coast of China in northeastern Hebei province. It features a long stretch of beach line, surrounded by mountains. On which marks the beginning of the Great Wall, and its first gate: Shanhai Guan.

The packaging design of Qinli Cake carries the purification of Qinhuangdao's culture. It symbolizes every historic scene spot and extracts the visual patterns by using line drawing. Hence, the packaging is like a magnificent picture—with beautiful landscape and imposing architecture, where golden iron horse galloping and waves running.

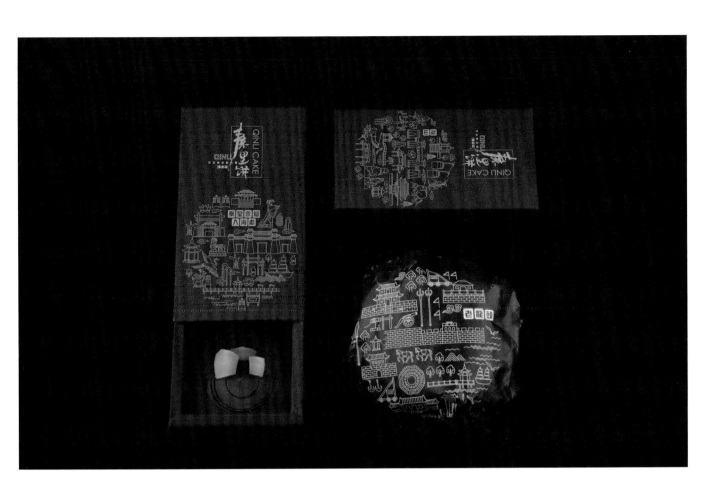

Three Mountains

Design: Yi-Hsuan Li

....

* Ink wash painting is an East Asian type of brush painting of Chinese origin that uses black ink—the same as used in East Asian calligraphy—in various concentrations. For centuries, this form of Chinese art was practiced by highly educated scholar gentlemen or literati.

Three Mountains is an art exhibition. The journey for artist is always feel like climbing countless mountains. They observe between themselves, their works and the world. They inquire about the essence, the meaning and the representation. On the long journey of searching, exploring and experiencing, they realize that art is more than a mountain, objectively. It is mist, vaguely. Artists are always on the way.

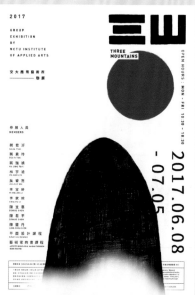

18 Lodgers

Design: AUCH Brand Design

....

Lingnan culture refers to the regional Chinese culture of the Southern Chinese twin provinces of Guangdong and Guangxi. It has become an influential cultural force in the international community, and forms the basis of the cultures of Hong Kong and Macau.

18 Lodgers is a hotel that filled with cultural and artistic boutiques, mix with exhibition, handicraft works, catering and lodging. Each brick and tile is rich in flavor of traditional culture. It allows visitors to taste the unique flavor of Lingnan culture.

Happy Monkey Year

Design: EARLYBIRDS DESIGN

* The Monkey is the ninth of the 12-year cycle of animals which appear in the Chinese zodiac related to the Chinese calendar.

In the year of the Monkey, designers use geometric shapes and lines to present the key visual of the monkey mask and card. This brings more fun and interactions. As for the gift box, there are bananas on it, so that the overall style can be consistent which make people feel warm and energetic.

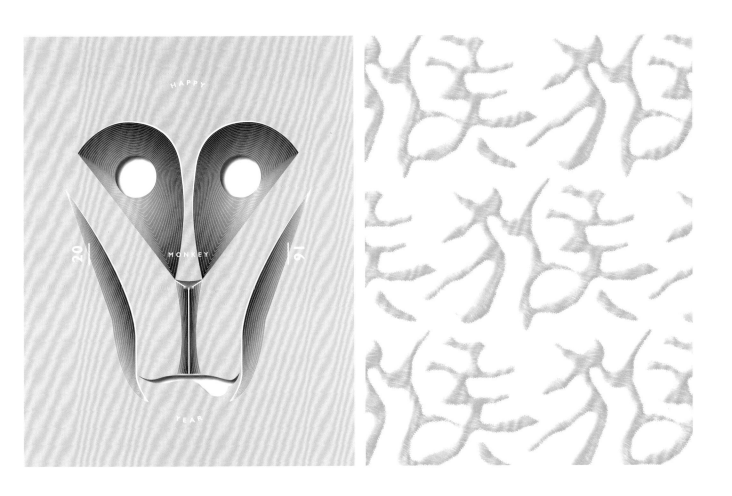

BLUSaigon

Design: GM creative   **Photography:** Nam Nguyen

* Ho Chi Minh City, also known by its former name of Saigon, is the largest city in Vietnam by population. Under the name Saigon, it was the capital of the French colony of Cochinchina and later of the independent republic of South Vietnam 1955-75.

Blu, an abbreviation of blue, is represents the ocean, which is the source of nacre for button-making family business years after years. Blue is also symbolizes the sky, where the sun and clouds appear, providing energy for every living thing on earth. Saigon is the name of Vietnam's famous city in 1861. BLUSaigon is associated with specific cultural and historical value of Vietnam, blended with the western culture.

Jakoten

Design: Grand Deluxe

....

* Furoshiki are a type of traditional Japanese wrapping cloth traditionally used to transport clothes, gifts, or other goods.

The design is for a famous local fish cake company. Since the first Chinese character of the company name appears to be a fish, the logo was designed to resemble a fish. The wave pattern on the bottom of the package represents the excellent fishery product. Consider the long history of the company, re-branding also included utilization of Japanese traditional culture, Furoshiki.

Xiang Tian Xia

Design: Guge dynasty

* Hot pot is a Chinese cooking method, prepared with a simmering pot of soup stock at the dining table, containing a variety of East Asian foodstuffs and ingredients. Different kinds of hot pots can be found in Sichuan.

Visually, Xiang Tian Xia chooses "Sichuan flavor" as its key point to present. People from all over the world are gather together for a Sichuan flavor dishes. Combining concept with graphics is adopted to create a brand image from an artistic perspective. It is about to spread the idea of "most delicious home flavor" to everyone.

Jin Tang Yu Lu

Design: Ideando

....

* This work is inspired by the Chinese ancient poets who live in seclusion. It tries to propagate their attitude towards life.

The whole design is launching around a poem: Glass bell, thick amber, crystal of Qiongtai, condense grace and elegance; essence collected, goods gathering, golden treasure of Yaochi, compete the enchanting flowers; a man indulged in the natural scenery, is like he owns the world.

The Happy 8

Design: 1983ASIA

This design is inspired by vibrant colors in local Malaysia, its mysterious national symbols as well as inclusive multiculture.

The Happy 8 is a high-quality chain hotels brand of Malaysia. The brand is enlightened from the combination of Nanyang culture and art. It re-interpreted national culture in an unique way, combined with the advantage of the other local hotels. The brand identity system has achieved a very strong coherent brand experience while giving uniqueness to every touch-points. Customers can experience a fabulous Nanyang culture and art in it—with hearts filled with joy, mutual respect and culture mixture.

Wu Fu Lin Men Gift Box

Design: Ideando

In Chinese, "Wu Fu Lin Men" means "five blessings have descended upon the house".

Wu Fu Lin Men is a design for new year gift box. "Fu" means blessings. The history of the Chinese nation is the history of people's pursuit of wealth and happiness. "Wu Fu", which is "five blessings" was first recorded in Shang Shu: "First blessing is the longevity, second is richness, third is health and peace, fourth is kindness, and fifth is natural death." And these are how Chinese defines "Fu".

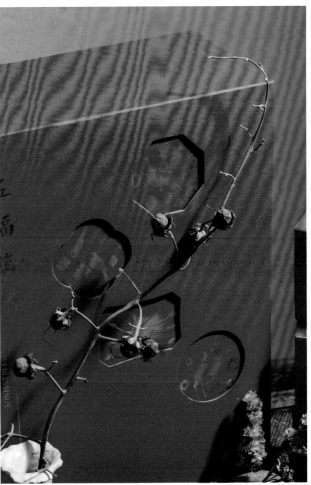

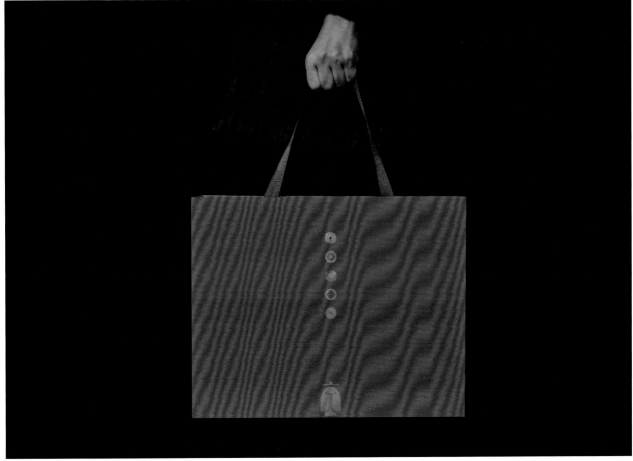

"Not Go Die" in the Year of the Dog

Design: LxU

* The Dog is eleventh of the 12-year cycle of animals which appear in the Chinese zodiac related to the Chinese calendar.

In the year of the Dog, LxU created the work "Not Go Die" (pronounced the same as "doggy bag" in Chinese), combining physical product with WebAR technology, to express thoughts and ideas for the problems that young generation were complaining about Chinese New Year. The work built AR animation in HTML5 and contained reserve meanings in graphic and animation designs: on the surface, it was used to avoid problems, but actually it was used to help people to understand each other better, and have a real happy new year. Scan the QR code to interact with the project.

Scarlet Jade of the East

Design: Shawn Goh Graphic Design Lab.

* Bakkwa, also known as rougan, is a Chinese salty-sweet dried meat product similar to jerky.

Chinese Bakkwa is a popular delicacy usually eaten during Chinese New Year. It is often used as a lavish gift to family and friends. The Chinese tradition of gift-giving can also be found in the Japanese gift-giving culture, "omiyage" or "temiyage". Hence, Japanese auspicious elements were shown in combination with Chinese oriented design. The gift box can pass new year wishes to the gift receivers and consumers.

Taipei Metro / 2018
Year of the Dog
Commemorative Tickets

Design: Midnight Design

* In Taiwan, China, "the wealth comes with a dog" means that fortunes come along when a homeless dog visits the house. In ancient times, it is not entirely a superstitious saying as only rich people could afford to have meat so that the smell of meat would attract the dogs. That is the saying comes from.

The cover is based on "the wealth comes with a dog", while the reverse side conveys "family reunion". The packaging design is to convey the meaning of "bring in (fortunes)". When opening the pack, the central structure will push the red pockets out of the package that indicates wealth comes along.

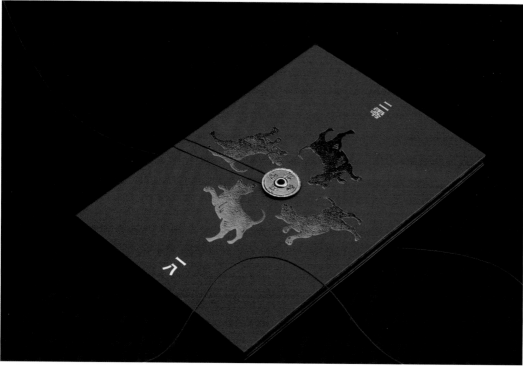

Chinese Intelligent Calendar 2018

Design: YOULIYOUJIE™

....

* The calendar contains four major parts, they are all about Chinese culture, such as festivals, solar terms, culture gene, and life wisdom. It covers festivals, architecture, life, entertainment and so on.

YOULIYOUJIE™ has spent 300 days to concentrate on the theme of "home", they carefully designed 377 illustrations. Each with original creativity. They also invent a "Chinese Intelligent Calendar" APP so that people can bring the "calendar" wherever they go and create themselves a personal calendar. There are dozens of key pages embedded AR technology, so people can scan their calendar pages with APP to experience the impressive audio, color, and dynamic.

Liberty Taiwanese Foods Pencil Series

Design: RIGHT BRAINS of RABBITS   **Photography:** Ting Lin

* This work applies traditional Taiwan snacks and Chinese lantern as the major visual elements.

Taiwan's multiculturalism creates many delicious and special snacks. Designers picture the snacks and also combine them with the image of traditional vendors. They try to make the students feel hungry when they study in class, writing homework, or sketching!

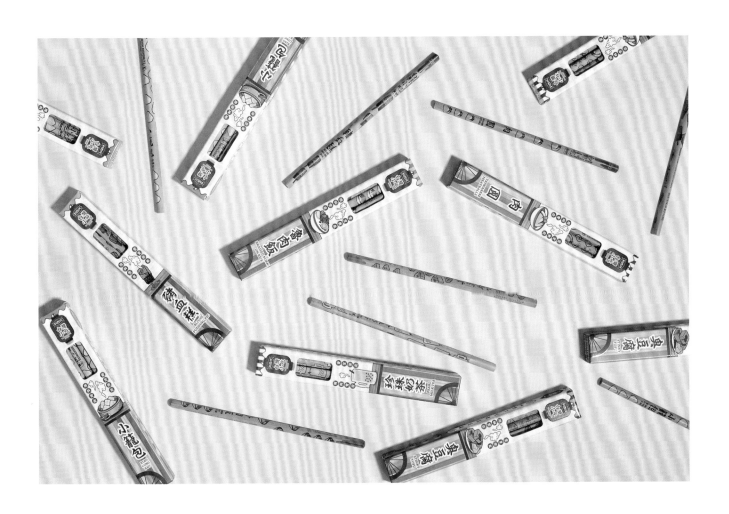

Year of Harmony Without Disputes

Design: Lien Chia-Hui   **Photography:** Plus Photography

"Protecting the Spiritual Environmental"
was the core philosophy brought up by Ven.
Master Sheng Yen, the founder of Dharma
Drum Mountain, in 1992.

The concept is aim to enhance the quality of humans, so humans are able to face reality and solve problems with healthy mentalities. The design element for the expression of visual design is focused on how lotus flowers and roots "grow out of mud yet remain pure and untainted", and based on this element, the imagery of spiritual purification is created.

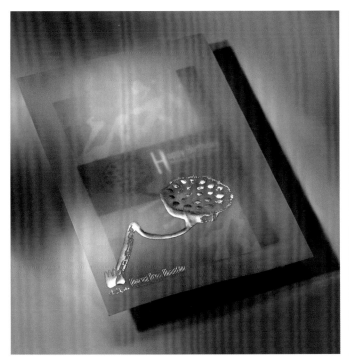

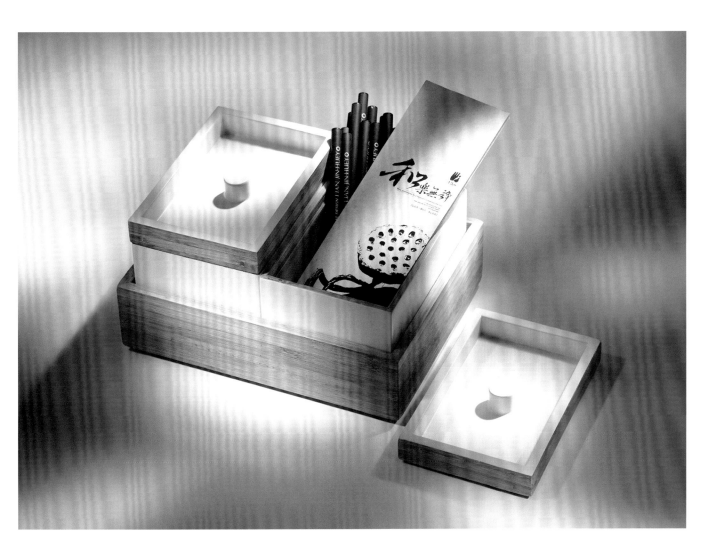

Qian Zhi Yu Ye
Royal Bird Tea

Design: Sun Shine

* Traditional animal patterns are the main visual elements in this work.

Qian Zhi Yu Ye Royal Bird Tea implies a bird bowed its head to sniff the local ancient tea. It indicates a natural scene that deep inside the forest, old trees are reaching to the sky, streams and rivers are chasing each other, birds are singing between the mountain, and fragrance of wild flowers is drifting. Royal Bird Tea is belonged to the eight famous tea in Qing Dynasty, it also served as the tribute tea to the royal court.

219

Forever Living Chinese New Year Angpao

Design: TSUBAKI

* Six blessings means longevity, richness, peace, good virtues, union, and filial piety. Angpao is also known as red packet.

This work is inspired by the "six blessings" which means prosperity and fortune. The angpao are decorated with curvy lines and Chinese ancient coin patterns that represent wealth. The purpose of making it a box set is to bring surprise and excitement to the recipient. It is usually inserted with money as a little token of "blessing" or "good luck" from the sender. During this auspicious occasion, it is very important to carry out the tradition of angpao with grace, respect and an open heart.

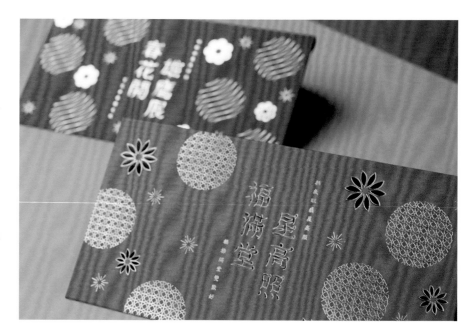

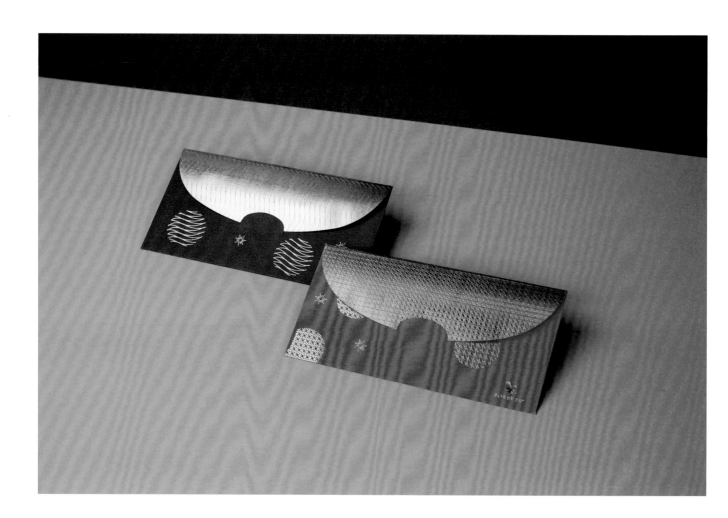

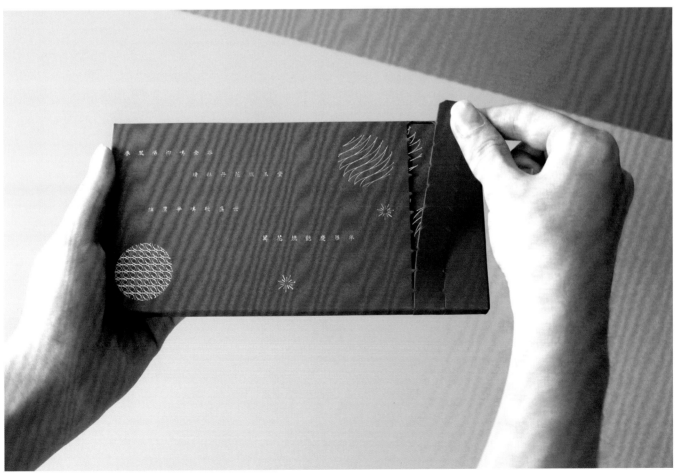

WU

Design: 1983ASIA

"Guan Bu" (means the attire specially designed for civil officials or military officer) is a best example in the Chinese totemism because it precisely interprets what "auspicious beast" means to Chinese people.

1983ASIA breaks the boundary of time and space. In the capacity of Asians, they refine the endless stories in "Guan Bu" and convert them into the "WU" series by designing some wonderful visual patterns. Through this work, they hope that the historical heritage won't die out but cherished by all people in the world.

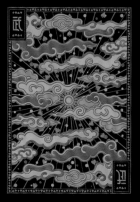

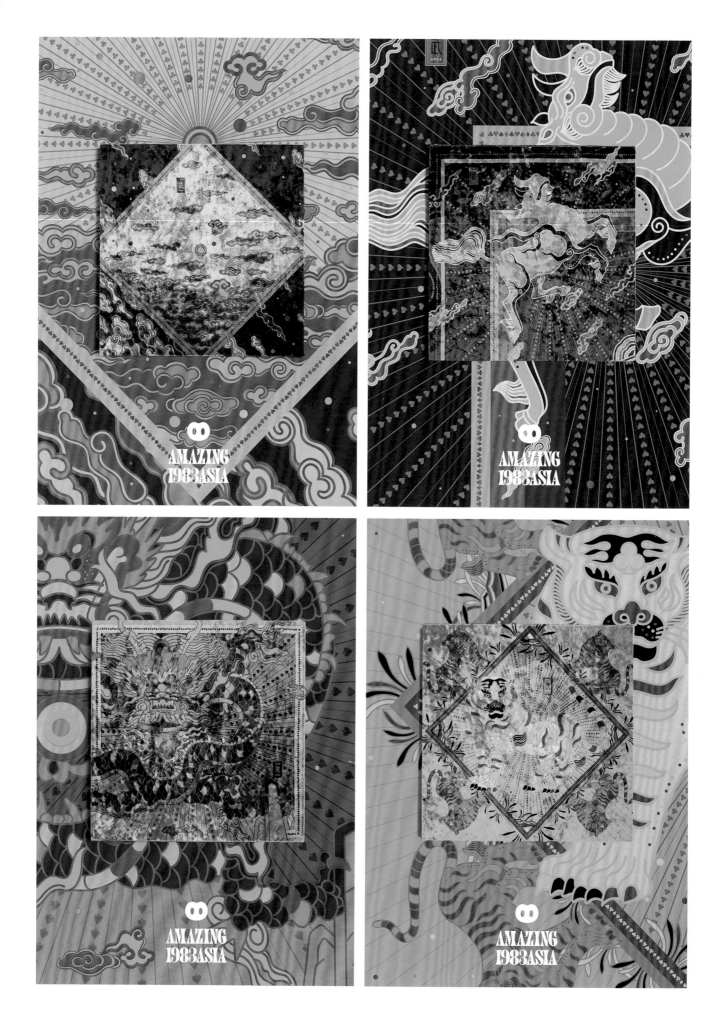

AMAZING
1983ASIA

AMAZING
1983ASIA

AMAZING
1983ASIA

AMAZING
1983ASIA

225

Singing Soil

Design: Hills Culture Communication

....

** Chinese folklore has it that humans were
originally created out of clay by the Goddess
Nüwa. Still using her simple materials, Chinese
folk artists revive this legend daily by molding
delicate clay figurines. In Ming Dynasty, clay
figurines came into their heyday and became
one of the most popular art forms.*

Singing Soil is a rebirth and tribute to
traditional folk handicrafts—clay figurines.
It is about to bring the audience back to the
connection with soil in childhood.

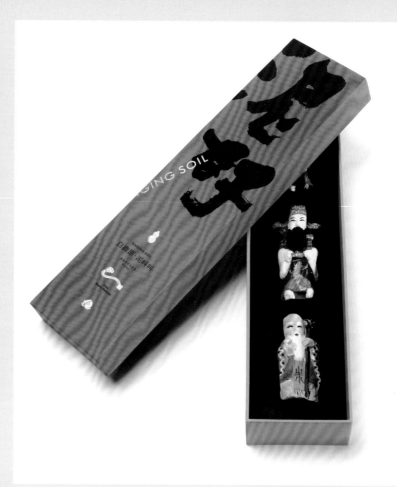

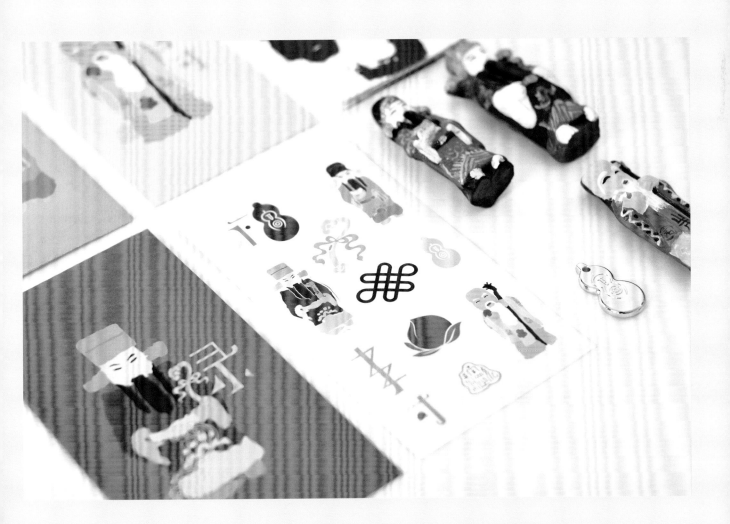

Wu Xing Theory

Design: NPFE PRESENTS

....

* The Wu Xing, also known as the Five Elements: Jupiter, Saturn, Mercury, Venus, Mars. It is a fivefold conceptual scheme that many traditional Chinese fields used to explain a wide array of phenomena, from cosmic cycles to the interaction between internal organs, and from the succession of political regimes to the properties of medicinal drugs. The "Five Elements" are Wood, Fire, Earth, Metal, and Water.

Wu Xing is an ancient philosophy in Chinese history. It is convinced that Wood, Fire, Earth, Metal, and Water are the abstract expression of this world. Wu Xing Theory is a book study the beginning of this world, and discuss the constant changes in life. The design and binding apply the rule of simplicity.

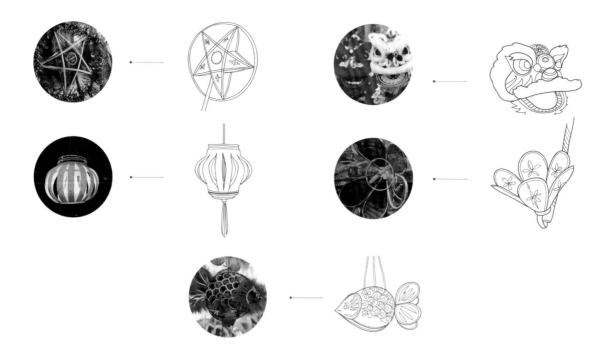

Lotte Hotels Resorts Moon Cake Box

Design: Incamedia   **Photography:** Incamedia

* This work uses lots of traditional elements of Mid-Autumn Festival to give a festive touch.

These illustrations are inspired from the distinctive Mid-Autumn Festival's items such as star lantern, handmade cans lantern, carp lantern, lion head, etc.

Hua Kai Fu Rong

Design: Guge dynasty

....

* Chengdu is a sub-provincial city which serves as the capital of Sichuan province. It is also known as the "Country of Heaven" and the "Land of Abundance".

This work takes Chengdu's hibiscus mutabilis as the artistic conception and the city prosperity as content. The rich cultural heritage and characteristic products are condensed into symbolic images, which sculpted in hibiscus mutabilis. The gift box is made of kraft paper, hemp rope and other ecological materials, which interprets the original ecology of agricultural products, and also shows the atmosphere of Chengdu humanities.

INDEX

2TIGERS design studio

2TIGERS design studio is a small multi-disciplinary design studio. Designers are aim to make things beautiful and fun. They create the design value of "suitable for the market and retain the unique taste of the brand" for customers, and then construct the brand value and generate the actual profit.

www.2tigersdesign.com

P128-131

9 × 9. Design

9 × 9. Design is mainly working on graphic visual image, brand image and communication, illustration, publication design and other services. They concentrate on the research and process, constantly break the conventions, and use unique visual language and thinking to renew the common elements in life. They spread visual information to customers and the public, and establish the emotional expression between people and design.

9×9.design

P060-061, 162-163

1983ASIA

1983ASIA was founded by Susu (China) and Yao (Malaysia) in Shenzhen, China. In 2017, they established Asia Aesthetics Institute focusing on Asia culture and art for graphic design. This unique combination leads the international mix art trends. 1983ASIA is a member of tDA Asia. Their works were displayed in London, Milan, Moscow, Berlin, Tokyo, and all over the world. They were awarded by Design for Asia Awards, Hong Kong Design Association, Global Design Awards and many more.

www.1983asia.com

P010-013, 030-031, 178-181, 184-185, 200-201, 222-225

ABCDESIGN

ABCDESIGN is a Hong Kong based design and branding studio. It provides full range of design services specialized in branding, identities, event identity, marketing strategy, packaging, print, publications and website design. It also provides solutions of photography, videography service. Designers believe their passion and creativity will bring energy to clients. They are a team of specialists of different professionals, designers, photographers, marketers. They work as a team to provide fresh ideas and brand solutions.

www.abcdesign.com.hk

P120-121

Adrienne Hugh

Adrienne Hugh is a visual creative from Hong Kong, and a recent graduate of the Rhode Island School of Design. Creating visually stimulating work across a variety of mediums, she strives to produce meaningful work.

adriennehugh.com

P150-151

And A Half Branding and Design Studio

And A Half is a brand consultancy and design studio based in Manila, Philippines, that builds brands and finds solutions with start-ups, corporations, and communities. The brand's designers are team to solve problems and create new forms of value. Their design process starts with their relationship with partners. Work gets done and gets done well through collaborative partnerships between designer and client. Both parties are equally engaged from beginning to end, with mutual respect for each others' thought processes. This keeps the work focused and honest, steadfast and authentic.

www.and-a-half.ph

P020-021

Andon Design Daily Co., Ltd.

Andon Design Daily Co.,Ltd. is a collective of enthusiastic designers who create experiences of real value that bring design to life. By understanding the fundamental of design, they always take the best solution from various inventive experimental processes. In a close partnership with clients, they help them to articulate their visions with creative purposeful outcome.

www.andondesigndaily.com

P096-097

Asia Chimian Company

Base on the background of consumption upgrading, Asia Chimian Company combines the superior resources of cultural and creative industries, facing consumers directly and transforming creativity into commercial value. It provides a fashionable and fun life and dining experience for the ethnic groups.

www.zcool.com.cn/u/14621502

P134-135

Asthetíque Group

Asthetíque Group is a multifaceted international design firm that created by Julien Albertini and Alina Pimkina. It harnesses its innate creativity and intuition to achieve distinguished works of art throughout various industries. Design is nonlinear in nature and being a dynamic company is essential when creating comprehensive projects.

www.asthetiquegroup.com

P094-095

AUCH Brand Design

AUCH Brand Design is a senior brand design organization in China. It provides brand strategy consultation, brand positioning, brand image creation and upgrading design, business interior design and brand marketing. It effectively promotes consumer's participation in brand building.

www.hkauch.com

P190-191

BEE DESIGN

BEE DESIGN is a new prominent design team from Xi'an. They believe that the future will be an era fulfilled with art. They pursues the things with soul, and their original design intention is to create things that valuable and artistic. BEE's self-expectation is to provide customers with super-value-added products, they hope to create their own future with the brand.

www.behance.net/bee_design

P108-109

Can Yang

Can Yang is a freelance graphic designer based in China. She graduated from Rhode Island School of Design in 2018 (BFA Graphic Design). She creates and pursues projects that situated between design and cultural communication, taken the practices of brand identity, interaction, editorial and conceptual art.

www.behance.net/canyang94

P112-113

Chieh-ting Lee

Chieh-ting Lee, graphic designer lives in Taipei, is majoring in commercial design in National Taiwan University of Science and Technology. He was awarded in 2015 Taiwan International Student Design Competition, Taiwan International Graphic Design Award, ASAKURA NAOMI Award, Shanghai Biennial Exhibition of Asia Graphic Design 2015, Macau Design Biennial award 2015, Blend-2015 International Typography Design Awards. Experimenting different materials and visual effects play an important role in his work.

www.behance.net/leechiehting

P052, 062-063

Dong Hoa Concept

Dong Hoa, literally means Oriental quintessence in Vietnamese. Dong Hoa Concept was founded by Quyen TN Le whom design strategy revolves around traditional patterns twisted with luxurious touch, and Thuan Hoang, whose creative graphic and packaging experience bring out the optimal blend of functional and opulent products. Their works are about to showcase remarkable Asian patterns with functional products.

www.behance.net/donghoacon2dfb

P080-081

EARLYBIRDS DESIGN

"The early bird represents beautiful beginning of every morning which is most full of energy and vitality, we insist that design is not only to create beauty and value, it is more like a most natural life attitude." EARLYBIRDS DESIGN was founded by Arron Chang and based in Taipei, through creative thinking and professional systematic plans, they create all kinds of unique brand images.

ebsdesign.com.tw

P192-193

Estudio Yeyé

Estudio Yeyé is a design studio focused on mix: brand identity, web, interior design, packaging, editorial design, illustration, art direction, digital design, environmental design... They preach the new world order of communication, the brands are their testament, they adore images that reflect truth and fight against false idols. The best way to tell the truth is through design. Design is truth, advertising is lying. They reject the old forms of marketing and embrace the teachings of design as the only language of the human creation.

yeye.design

P022-025, 136-139, 174-175, 182-183

Fan Shuilun

Graduated from the Hong Kong Polytechnic University, Fan Shuilun now works as a communication designer in Hong Kong.

www.fanshuilun.com

P092-093

GM creative

GM stands for "Gao-Muoi" in Vietnamese language. It hopes to make ends meet and bring their heart and soul through their products.

gaomuoicreative.com

P032-033, 194-195

Grand Deluxe

Grand Deluxe is a graphic design studio based in Ehime, Japan, which was founded in 2005 by Koji Matsumoto. It is the winner of various awards such as ONE SHOW Gold, New York ADC Silver, D&AD Bronze, and Pentawards Silver.

www.grand-deluxe.com

P196

Guge dynasty

Guge dynasty is a well-known brand design consultancy organization in China's food industry. Since its establishment in 2002, it has collaborated with the top 500 food enterprises in China and the world, and achieved an overall output value of more than 100 billion yuan. Guge dynasty has won the WorldStar Award, Pentawards Gold Award, Red Dot Best Outstanding Design Award and so on.

www.ycguge.com

P168, 197, 232

Hills Culture Communication

Hills Culture Communication has been devoted to the research and exploration in the field of design and art. It has stepped into the multi-dimensional world of plane design, commercial space and product design, and has been active in various kinds of design and art exhibitions, trying to break the boundaries of art, design and life.

www.jianshan816.com

P099, 226-227

Hoa Nguyen (AJ)

Hoa Nguyen (AJ) is a Vietnamese multidisciplinary designer, working on brand identity and print graphic.

Ajnguyen.com

P018

Hong-Wun Lu

Hong-Wun Lu, a graphic designer, specializes in visual image, font design, poster design, etc. He participated in the proposal of World Expo Museum logo in Shanghai in 2014. He won many international design awards. He is the author of The Research on the Viewpoints of International Poster Design.

www.behance.net/LuHongWun

P070-071

Huang Yufang

Huang Yufang comes from a small town in the center of Taiwan, China, where the old house is next to the mountains and lakes. She now resides in Taipei city and lives a busy life. No matter traditional or contemporary, artistic or commercial, separated or follow the mainstream, she tries her best to make a variety of entanglements.

www.behance.net/letterofcat

P088-089

Hue Studio

Hue Studio is an Australian based design studio. Founded by Vian Risanto in 2005, Hue Studio specialises in creative design and brand development for the hospitality, architecture and commercial sector. They love to solve problems with creativity, create effective and tailored design solutions that attract, engage and inspire.

www.huestudio.com.au

P026-027

Ideando

Ideando is a creative and executive design studio. They providing design consulting services to all types of customers, analyzing the language conception, defining the concept, providing the design, and clarifying the need for accurate positioning.

www.behance.net/Idea-and-do

P198-199, 202-203

i'll studio

i'll studio shares the emotions with everyone through its art and design. It creates collectible belongings that represented/expressed the audience.

www.fb.com/iwillstudio

P164-165

Incamedia

Founded in 2006, Incamedia began as a team of young, dynamic and passionate designers and creatives, and is now one of the leading design firms in Vietnam. Serving some of the biggest companies and groups in Vietnam, as well as international brands operating in the country, Incamedia offers fresh and innovative design and printing solutions.

www.incamedia.vn

P158-159, 230-231

just-o studio

just-o studio is founded by creative duo who are really passion about design and branding, and they have built brand identities for many local business over the years. They believe design is a process of creating meaningful works that can make an impact or difference to those see them.

www.behance.net/JustOStudio

P154-155

KittoKatsu

Established in 2015, KittoKatsu is a small agency specializing in brand strategy and design. They work with a broad range of clients from individuals and institutions to local business and global brands. They believe in strong brand management as the essential steering instrument for companies. That is why, in each project KittoKatsu aims to combine brand strategy and design, developing the brand personality together with their clients and then transforming it into a unique visual identity.

www.kittokatsu.de

P016-017, 160-161

La Come Di

La Come Di is a fashion label based in Dubai. Their unique style is made of electric graphic and color blocking elements that stand against anything mainstream. With experiences that vary from design, art direction, photography and illustration, La Come Di is a product of passion and connection to different stories that people will touch and feel in their designs.

www.lacomedi.com

P072-073

Langcer Lee

Langcer Lee is a designer based in Tianjin, China. He engaged in brand design for years. He is the winner of Golden Pin Design Award, GBDO, Beijing Gift, ZCOOL Award 2018 and many more. He is also the founder of LITETE Brand Design, a company that provides design services for hundreds of enterprises. Its business service is throughout the country and overseas.

www.behance.net/Langcer

P169

Li Jialing

Li Jialing is a visual designer base in Shanghai and Taipei. Studying in the Institute of Design in National Taiwan University of Science and Technology, he is skilled in typography and font art.

www.behance.net/lee-SH

P014-015

Lien Chia-Hui

Lien Chia-Hui acts as the Creative Director of Yi Jia Visual Identity Design Co.,Ltd. now. She is also the director of the design center of Tung Fang Design University and an assistant professor of arts and crafts. Her professional fields of design include brand design, graphic design, packaging design, book design, and exhibition visual design. She designs various projects for customers from each and all sections. She also been honored many awards.

www.facebook.com/superpolly0217

P216-217

Lilly Ark, Atcharani Thanabun, Jiang Pei-Xuan, Li Zi-Xuan, Xu Si-Ying, and Gao Li-Ting

Team works by six visual communication design students, this work was exhibited in Kaohsiung, Taipei, Taiwan, 2017.

www.behance.net/LilyArk

P144-147

Lu Qifang

Lu Qifang is a freelance illustrator whose character is as warm as cat, he is easy-going and curious about the world. His illustrations starting from his unique absurd youth, with boundless imagination, he shows the audience a full and warm, free-flowing style.

luqifang.lofter.com

P098

LxU

LxU is an innovative company of content marketing and design.

www.lxustudio.com

P204-205

Margaret Cheung

Graduated from Hong Kong Design Institute and Department of Visual Communication in Birmingham City University, Margaret Cheung was majored in brand design. Now she works as a graphic designer and mainly focus on developing brand image and Chinese font design.

www.ckymdesign.com

P034-035

MAROG Creative Agency

MAROG Creative Agency based in Yerevan, Armenia offers advertising, branding and graphic design, events management services to local and international companies.

www.marog.co

P038-039

MC BRAND

MC BRAND focuses on the value of the brand. Adhering to the refined research attitude towards target consumer groups, they provide a set of business innovation services for enterprises, such as business model research, target customer group research, industry innovation positioning, marketing structure combing, and operation suggestions.

m.mc-vi.com

P074-075

Mengchia Hu

Mengchia Hu is a graphic designer. She likes to create in various forms, especially in cultural themes. Design and creation are parts of her life. Through design, she can understand herself better. She convinced the essence of design is not only to create beautiful things, but also to solve more problems.

reurl.cc/xE94e

P104-105

Miao Shou Hui Chao

Miao Shou Hui Chao is aim to renovate Chinese traditional culture from a young perspective, to transform culture into design content, and to export essence to ordinary people in various ways. They want to link modern life with Chinese traditional culture.

www.mshc2018.com

P019, 058-059

Midnight Design

A team of talented designers from various fields. They devote themselves to brainstorm and interweave creative ideas all through the night for dynamic and extraordinary designs. Midnight Design dedicate their time to solve dilemmas for clients, they accomplish the mission through unique perspectives and dynamic analysis. They value the reliance and the request from every client for integrating both thoughts to achieve a satisfied result.

www.behance.net/designinmidnight

P208-209

National Taichung University of Science and Technology

Team members include Ku Pei-Wen, Chiou Yu-Ching, Shih Mei-Ju, Weng Ching-Te, and Yang Po-Zhi. They graduated from National Taichung University of Science and Technology, and were majored in graphic, illustration, packaging design.

www.behance.net/gallery/64591393/-Oh-Oh-Pressure-Go

P114-115

NPFE PRESENTS

NPFE PRESENTS is a leading brand commercial design company empathizing in creativity. They assist growing businesses to create unique and differentiated brand designs. NPFE PRESENTS specializes in re-branding, marketing and public relations, brand design, product and packaging design, as well as publishing. They are experts zing in serving global business creativity through effective and rapid information acquisition, conversion, multi-dimensional integrated communication and efficient implementation of service capabilities.

www.npfe.cn

P228-229

ONE & ONE DESIGN

ONE & ONE DESIGN is focusing on brand integration, brand packaging, visual design and some other field. They believe in using their professional skills to create the original and innovative design works. They hope to create wonderful brand systems for clients through their scientific, effective and internationalization design.

www.behance.net/1and1design

P086-087

Oscar Bastidas

Oscar Bastidas is a Venezuelan art director, specialized in branding design. He now lives in Brooklyn, New York. Oscar has over 11 years of experience on the development of advertising material and art pieces. He is also known as "Mor8". Currently, his artwork is booming amongst emerging brands from numerous industries in different countries.

mor8graphic.com

P040-041

Paperlux Studio

Paperlux Studio, established since 2006, is an eclectic mix of branding experts, designers, material fetishists and project wizards focused on digital and print communication tools. Their designs and craft evolve in an environment that combines studio, office and workshop for, and especially in partnership with, German and international brands. Their heart and home can be found in Hamburg's dynamic Schanzenviertel district.

paperlux.com

P036-037

Pengguin

Pengguin is a multidisciplinary design studio based in Hong Kong. Founded by the design duo—Todd and Soho, who believe in good design should always gives a positive energy and visual satisfaction. They are also good storytellers, keening on sharing different story and concept by catching the chemistry between space and visual context.

pengguin.hk

P153

RIGHT BRAINS of RABBITS

RIGHT BRAINS of RABBITS creates design by using the right brain emotional thinking. They emphasis on creative thinking, and adhere to the beauty of the design and the requirements of the quality. They strive to achieve the aesthetic objective optimization.

rabbits.com.tw

P214-215

Rong Brand

Rong Brand was founded in 2009. It emphasizes on positioning and aesthetics, pays attention to commercial effect as well as national aesthetics. Instead of "pointing the way" high above and "entertain" the designer's personal will, Rong Brand "fighting" with the market in its solid and effective way.

https://www.behance.net/rongbrand0cf3

P056-057, 064-065

ROYU Brand Design

Established in 2006, ROYU Brand Design shaped the brand with feelings and advocated as the main purpose. Over 10 years, it concentrated on the creation and promotion of brand image and brand service. Its profound professional philosophy and perfect operating system not only gain the trust and praises of many clients, but also win over 100 professional awards in many kinds.

www.rongyu06.com

P082-083, 176-177, 186-187

SAFARI inc.

Established by Tomoki Furukawa and Jyun Ogita in 2003, SAFARI inc. engages in art direction and design in various fields from corporate or product branding, packaging, editorial, web and space production. The company name of "SAFARI" means "adventure" in Arabic. It expresses their desire of "keep cherishing curiosity forever and ever".

www.safari-design.com

P124-125

SanYe Design Associates

Through SanYe Design Associates' visual comprehension, they bring out the aesthetic in brand. And with the accumulation of aesthetic and culture experience, they transfer such perceptual power into their products and package design, creating brand identity; and further, lighting up the three core values which visual design endues with to the brand image: the values in aesthetic, cultural significance, and the ability to move one's heart.

www.3yadesign.com

P132-133

Shawn Goh Graphic Design Lab.

Since its establishment in 2014, Shawn Goh Graphic Design Lab. has emerged to be one of the top design companies in Malaysia. It has received recognition

from various design associations on both national and international levels. Some of the awards received include Italy, Korea and German. Original, unique, customized and innovative design is the biggest promise to their valuable clients.

www.behance.net/Shawngoh

P206-207

Sun Shine

After 11 years of efforts, Sun Shine has become one of the well-known design companies in China. Many successful cases have a strong impact on the market. Although it is based in Guizhou, the mountains do not stop the designers from pursuing the dream, on the contrary, Guizhou has continued to give them unique and precious inspiration. The cultural nutrients make them different.

www.sunsund.com

P068-069, 218-219

Ta Quang Huy

Ta Quang Huy is a young designer comes from Vietnam. He loves books and pizza. He often takes both at once.

huytadesign.com

P046-047

The Box Brand Design Ltd.

The Box Brand Design Ltd. is a team focus on thinking and execution. Brain storming and diverse ideas are what they passion about. Box believes that strategy is not listed of theories from the textbook. In fact, they analysis and dig into the client core value of their business by following brand principles. As a result, clients can carry out the steps with concrete implementation plans.

www.boxbranddesign.com

P166-167, 170-171

The Creative Method

The Creative Method was established in 2005 with a sole purpose of creating the highest quality design solutions underpinned by even better ideas. The focus has and always will be on creating brands that have impact, standout, a point of difference and most importantly brands that work.

www.thecreativemethod.com

P090-091

Thinking*Room

Thinking*Room is a design company based in Jakarta, Indonesia. Through their intuitive approach and crafted skills they have used both traditional and non-traditional methods to communicate the different elements of brand. They serve full-design-service, focus on brand identities, strategy, campaign, content creation, products and packaging, books, websites, social media, motion, interiors, exhibition, installations, environments, and more.

thinkingroominc.com

P140-141

TICK.DESIGN

TICK.DESIGN was established in 2015. It strives to create inspiring visual experience and one-of-a-kind design for clients. They provide brand analysis and market evaluation for varied design cases, discovering core brand spirit, and executing design project. Their tailor made design plan will leverage the accuracy of the brand's creativity execution and enhance brand personality, with unique attractiveness and creativeness.

www.tick-design.com

P044-045

TOMSHI AND ASSOCIATES

TOMSHI AND ASSOCIATES is a multi-disciplinary creative studio focusing on integrated user experience. They offer visual solutions and apply design thinking to a wide range of areas, like brand identity, retail space design, window design and installation, packaging, product design, etc.

www.tomshi.com

P110-111, 116-117, 122-123

TSUBAKI

TSUBAKI is a Japanese word for camellia, the flower associated with good luck. As a creative boutique agency, TSUBAKI has grown leaps and bounds in the span of ten years, specialising in branding and visual communications. TSUBAKI was set up in 2007 by Jay Lim and Vivian Toh, and has won more than 15 international design awards in recent years.

www.tsubakistudio.net

P220-221

UNIDEA BANK

Everyone is a product design company with "strategy as the guide, visual expression as the means, and product landing as the goal". UNIDEA BANK is good at mining the "invisible value" of products, restoring the "value of the goods"; promoting the upgrading of local brands with an international perspective, and promoting appropriate design.

www.unidea-bank.com

P066-067

Victor Branding Design Corp.

Since the foundation in 1988, Victor Branding Design Corp. sets up mission in "Your Design Partners" by gathering talents of relevant fields with commitment in online image design, graphic design, packaging design, website design and consultant, forming into a multi-dimensional professional integration service team.

www.victad.com.tw

P042-043, 048-049, 172

Wang Fugui Design

The original intentions of Wang's design is hope the world will become better. He is willing to provide free design for some commonweal organizations, some normal pedlar and small workshops. He hopes everyone can enjoy the better design.

www.wangfugui1984.lofter.com

P118-119

Xiaoyue Liu

Xiaoyue Liu is a designer and illustrator currently resident in New York City. She was born and raised in mainland China.

xiaoyueliu.com

P050-051

Xu Rui

Xu Rui is an independent graphic designer. He was a postgraduate majored in Visual Communication, Tsinghua University. His works were selected to participate in many exhibitions, and won lots of awards.

weibo.com/u/5770271525

P102-103

XY Creative

XY Creative sets up in Beijing. It strives to develop a more young and professional brand service.

www.xycreative.cn

P156-157

Yang Quanwen (TOOZ)

Yang Quanwen is a designer of TOOZ. In TOOZ, designers are engaged in brand design and research, they are good at excavating and shaping brand exclusive culture and planning design. Distinctive in style, they also build up brand personality from design and form the brand differentiation.

www.behance.net/457283407ef78

P152

Yi-Hsuan Li

Yi-Hsuan is a Taiwanese visual designer specializes in minimalist and eastern design style. She always engages in designs with combing traditional and modern element to express a different view with her special esthetic experience. Her designs have won "Adobe Design Achievement Award", "Golden Pin Concept Design Award 2016", Merit Award of "DFA Design for Asia Awards 2016" and so on.

www.yihsuanli.com

P028-029, 142-143, 188-189

YINGSHI & FASHENG

YINGSHI & FASHENG takes the brand strategy as the core and aims to solve problem. It focuses on the brand's construction and management. Based on the observation and study of Chinese market and local consumers, they constantly explore the "sensory" in graphic design and "strategic" in marketing.

www.gtn9.com/user_show.
aspx?id=9DD7F0E81B887590

P106-107

Yosuke Ando

Yosuke Ando is a freelance graphic designer currently based in Tokyo, Japan, whose work focuses on typography and illustration. He spent most of his life in Sydney, Australia and has worked with Luca Ionescu of Like Minded Studio and then as a designer at M&C Saatchi.

www.yske.net

P173

YOULIYOUJIE™

Established in 2014, YOULIYOUJIE™ has built up a product system includes aspects of life, culture, education and festivals. At the same time, they systematize the process of brand research, promotion, supplication, and warehouse allocation, and have grown into a representative Chinese cultural brand.

www.behance.net/yimixiaoxin

P100-101, 126-127, 210-213

Yusuke Yamazaki

Yusuke Yamazaki is a Toronto based graphic designer. He was born and raised in Shizuoka, Japan. He designs with precision and proficiency, using cross-cultural design knowledge to create diverse pieces of work that will shape ordinary interactions into meaningful experiences.

www.behance.net/yusukey

P076-079

Zhang Han

Zhang Han works as a creative director in Yang Zhongli Marketing (Shanghai/Guangzhou/Wuhan). He is the member of SGDA. He adheres to the "extraordinary initiative" work and also good at visual creation of "graphic line type". From the three levels of strategy, content, and vision, he explores new and appropriate commercial innovation programs.

www.behance.net/zhanghandesign

P053, 054-055

Zhang Haocheng

Zhang Haocheng is a young visual designer and a photographer. His poster works have been collected in BICeBe 2017 and Korean Ensemble of Contemporary Design.

www.behance.net/zhanghawso20b2v

P084-085

Zhang Xiaoning

Zhang Xiaoning is a new prominent designer. He is good at brand and packaging design. He advocates a balance between commercial value and artistry in design. He was addicted to the collision and combination of Chinese traditional elements and modern design. He also has a strong foresight.

zxn-design.com

P148-149

ACKNOWLEDGEMENTS

We would like to express our gratitude to all of the designers and companies for their generous contribution of images, ideas, and concepts. We are also very grateful to many other people whose names do not appear in the credits but who made specific contributions and provided support. Without them, the successful compilation of this book would not be possible. Special thanks to all of the contributors for sharing their innovation and creativity with all of our readers around the world.